# FRIEND ENCYCLOPEDIA

### YOUR GUIDE TO FRIEND TYPES AND HOW TO DEAL WITH THEM

## PAULA HOLLAND

DUNAMIS MEDIA GROUP

# CONTENTS

# 1

## DEDICATION

This book is dedicated to the Late Shanquella Robinson, a beautiful young woman with a promising future that was cut short by her so-called friends. It is also dedicated to others who have sadly left this world without having had the pleasure of experiencing faithful and loyal friends and to those still living who are on the quest to find them.

# INTRODUCTION

True friendship is one of the most rewarding relationships one can experience in a lifetime. The problem is that we aren't formally taught in school what a friend is or how to make friends. Sure, we're given some basic instructions about sharing with others and we're taught not to hit one another as early as preschool and kindergarten. But there is no detailed curriculum on friendship taught in K-12 schools or advanced friendships at the university level, not even in psychology classes. So how does one navigate the friendship landscape and learn how to attract the right friends, how to spot the questionable or wrong ones, and what to do about them? For most people, this amounts to guess work or advice from people who are blindly plodding through life as they are.

I am one of those people who navigated the landscape of friendships on my own, and at times it felt like a battlefield. How I wished there had been a manual to spell out for me what to look for in a good friend and how to spot the losers and dangerous people masquerading as friends. Unfortunately, I had to figure out these things on my own.

Back in 2011, I decided to categorize what I had learned about friends; the good and the bad, and share them with others, and this is how the *Friend Encyclopedia* was born.

A friend can be closer and dearer than a member of one's own blood family, but a wrong friend can do irreparable damage to your very soul. We recently saw this play out in October 2022 with the late Shanquella Robinson, a young woman who was murdered by people she considered to be her close friends. I would bet my last dollar that there had been signs that these 'so-called friends' had shown Shanquella, but because she had likely never received any formal training on what a friend is and is not, she missed those signs and it ended up costing her in an irreparable way.

While not having an understanding of what a friend is and is not is usually not fatal, it can still leave emotional scars. My mother once told me a story about an incident involving a friend of my grandmother's that deeply affected my grandmother for life.

My mother was a young girl at the time of this incident. My grandmother and a woman my grandmother considered to be a good friend went to the movies and took with them my mother and my aunt, who were children at the time.

As they all stood in line to pay for tickets, my grandmother's friend, who I will call 'Margaret' realized that she was missing a dollar bill. She immediately blamed my grandmother for the missing dollar, called her names, and vehemently accused her of stealing the money out of her purse.

My grandmother denied the accusation and the two women got into a heated argument that quickly escalated into a shouting match.

Suddenly, Margaret reached into her own coat pocket and found the dollar bill. It seemed she had only misplaced the money, but instead of apologizing to my grandmother for the mistake, Margaret suggested they just see the movie and acted as if nothing had just happened.

My grandmother's feelings were hurt that her friend would not only assume that she would have done something so low as to steal from her, but that Margaret had accused her and called her names. To make matters worse, Margaret never apologized.

According to my mother, my grandmother moped around the house crying for days. When she finally stopped grieving about what had happened, she declared to the family that not only would she no longer be friends with Margaret but she didn't want to have any more friends ever again.

My grandmother's declaration sounded pretty drastic to me. As a kid growing up, I don't ever recall my grandmother having friends over to the house or participating in activities with anyone I would call friends. She pretty much kept her activities to what we did in our family or going to work.

When I attended church with my grandmother, I observed her being cordial with everyone and there certainly were ladies of the church that she was friendly towards as they worked together in various ministries. But true to her word, my grandmother did not have any close friends and that remained the case until the day she died.

It made me sad that one wrong friend hurt my grandmother so profoundly that she made such a drastic decision to never have friends again. I've always wondered how a few good friends might have positively impacted my grandmother's life had she cast aside what had happened with Margaret and allowed good friends in.

Over the course of my life, I've experienced a range of friendships from really amazing to unbelievably horrific. I know firsthand, the sheer joy that comes from having a faithful friend you can count on as well as the excruciating pain that comes from having a wrong friend.

My goal for writing *Friend Encyclopedia* is to equip readers with the insights I've gained over the years about good and not-so-good friends and how to deal with them while navigating the friendship landscape as a whole. For additional insight on the subject of friendship and many other self-help topics, visit my website at friendencyclopedia.com, sign up for my free newsletter, and check out other helpful resources. I'd love to hear from you about your thoughts on friendship, other friend types I may have missed, or ideas you have on friendship. Feel free to get in touch with me from the contact tab on my website!

# 3

## How Friend Encyclopedia Came to Be

It started out so innocently. I was engaged in a Yahoo Groups session for one of many groups to which I belonged and was about to log out when I noticed a Yahoo Answers member asking a question about a situation with a friend. Curious, I clicked on the link and answered the question. To me, the answer seemed like a no-brainer.

Once I had answered the first question, several more friend-related questions popped up for me to answer. It was a little addictive and I found myself spending hours answering question after question until I finally pushed myself away from the computer.

As I thought about several of the questions posed by a variety of age groups from tweeners up through adults, it dawned on me that there were a lot of people out there who were having a tough time deciphering friendship.

A few days later, I began receiving notifications from Yahoo Answers that several of my answers had been selected as winners. I logged back into Yahoo Answers and began answering more friend-related questions. Again, I continued receiving winning notifications and realized that I might be on to something. As I went back and reviewed some of the other user answers that had not been selected, I was amazed by how many responses were so far off the mark, in my opinion.

For the most part, I don't think it was a matter of trolls plugging in a slew of fake answers to incite emotions, but rather there are a lot of people out there who really don't have a clue about the true meaning of friendship and yet they are navigating through life, entangling themselves into the lives of others and engaging in what they call friendship but oftentimes is not.

Earlier in life, I stood in the shoes of one who did not have a clue about what a friend was and I was often on the receiving end of bad treatment. To my shame, there have also been times in my past when I was not a good friend.

Looking back at my years in elementary, junior high, and high school, I never took a single class that taught me how to be a friend or how to make friends. I don't recall seeing any friend courses in college, and believe me, I looked. I never once saw any 'friend' curriculum in Sociology or Psychology classes that I'd examined. I've asked several people about their experiences when it comes to learning how to make friends, and the answers were the same as mine – no one had taken classes to learn how to be or how to make friends.

I believe most of us just sort of navigate life, showing ourselves friendly toward those we like and hoping for the best. If we're lucky, we have a family member that may give us a few good tips on how to make friends. You can also find books that advise about dealing with bullies and how to influence people but nothing about categorizing friend types and how to navigate them.

My mom used to always tell me that if I wanted to have friends, then I'd have to show myself friendly. It was good advice but I always struggled with exactly what that meant especially when it came to wrong friends with questionable character traits. Fortunately, most of my experiences with showing myself friendly worked out pretty well. In other instances, they were disastrous and I made a lot of mistakes along the way.

So, what makes me an expert in the area of friendship? It's simple. I've learned from my myriad mistakes, analyzed what went right or wrong, how it could have been remedied or prevented, and went back to the drawing board until I learned to successfully navigate the friendship landscape, resulting in me having quality friendships in a variety of friend types. My professional experience in the field of marketing and communications, and working in research departments didn't hurt either.

I have hands-on experience with nearly every friend type in this book and have slogged my way through fruitless and at times, toxic relationships, as well as having the pleasure of encountering high-quality friends. I've gained a solid understanding of what to look for in a friend you are considering for a close friendship, as well as how to be one. It is my pleasure to share my insights with anyone genuinely looking to make or to be a quality friend.

*Friend Encyclopedia* is written in a quick reference style for easy reading and provides detail about a variety of positive, neutral, and negative friend types that I've placed in 3 categories:

Positive friends that you should proactively pursue, I refer to as, "***Green light friends***".

1. Friends that you should proceed with cautiously, I refer to as "*Yellow light friends*".

2. And friends that you should strongly consider <u>not</u> proceeding with but should exit the relationship as quickly and safely as possible, I refer to as "*Red light friends*".

There are a total of 27 friend types detailed in the following chapters. While I am sure that there are more than 27 friend types, I am confident that most friends you will encounter will fall somewhere within these 27 types.

It is worth noting that these friend types can also be applied to work relationships and even romantic relationships. When it comes to successful romantic relationships, the good ones that have lasting power are based on solid friendships, and you'll find many of these listed in the positive friend type section. I'll touch on romantic relationships a bit more in the Purpose of Friendship chapter that you will find as soon as you turn this page!

# 4

## The Purpose of Friendship

I am a firm believer that it is important to know the purpose of a thing before engaging with it. Without knowing something's purpose, how can you possibly use it correctly or use it to its full potential? This principle of knowing the purpose of something definitely applies to friendship.

As I see it, the purpose of friendship is two-fold: the first is for you to bring positive elements to another person to enrich his or her life and the second is for that same person to bring positive elements to your life in a manner that elevates both of you in the relationship, as well as your individual lives; it's knives sharpening knives.

In this respect, friendship can be compared to a hearty soup. A basic hearty soup is made up of vegetable or meat broth as the base, vegetables, a variety of spices, and sometimes meat.

In a friendship, both parties must contribute to the making of this proverbial soup. Sometimes, both parties are not always contributing equally to the soup at the same time. Unfortunately, things happen in life. If a friend experiences a great loss such as the loss of a close family member or a job, he or she might contribute less and take more from the friendship. However, under normal circumstances, being a constant taker and rarely giving back is not a good dynamic.

If you are the one providing the broth base as well as the meat, the vegetables, and the spices while your friend routinely contributes nothing but always shows up to eat the soup, then you have a one-sided relationship that will eventually be very unsatisfying for you and you will grow to resent that friend. The same goes for you if you are doing all the taking and contributing little or nothing under normal circumstances. Ideally, in this situation, you and your friend would both generously contribute.

Before I began writing *Friend Encyclopedia*, I spoke with several people of all ages and found that many have been in friendships where, like my soup example, they were providing all of the ingredients while their friend provided very little or the friend contributed bad ingredients that made the soup inedible or toxic.

Friendships are foundational relationships that are the launching pad for other types of relationships, especially romantic ones.

Healthy romantic relationships that I have witnessed that have lasting power are built on a solid foundation of friendship. Like a well-built house that has a solid and even foundation, these healthy romantic relationships were first founded on good friendship before the relationship blossomed into something more significant.

# 5

## HOW THIS BOOK WORKS

*Friend Encyclopedia* details 27 friend types that are separated into three categories that include positive friends (**Green light**), neutral friends (**Yellow light**), and negative friends (**Red light**). Many of these friend types revolve around work relationships and some could even translate into romantic relationships.

If you are currently in a romantic relationship or are considering entering one, pay close attention to the positive friend category since this is where you will likely want to draw evaluations from.

All 27 friend types are detailed in a specific format that includes a short story about fictitious friends followed by:

- Pros of the friend type

- Cons of the friend type

- How to deal with the friend type

- What if you <u>are</u> this friend type

Each of the 27 friend types follows this model detailed above which should make it easy to scan for a friend type and find advice on how to deal with someone who has these particular traits.

Not every person will fit cleanly into a particular friend type. You may find that some people that resemble one friend type may also have secondary traits that place them in another type as well. The point is to provide a general reference that someone in question may fit.

Following the 27 friend types, there is a chapter called "A Good FFIT" that provides information on what to look for in high-quality friends and how to become one.

# 6

## GREEN LIGHT FRIENDS

# 7

## FUN COMMITTEE MEMBERS

*L*auren met Tammy at a party of a mutual friend. Tammy seemed really cool. She was funny, witty, and liked to drink as hard as Lauren did. The two women, both in their early 30s, exchanged mobile numbers and agreed to hang out again.

Sure enough, right before the following weekend, Tammy called Lauren and invited her to go bar hopping. On that Friday evening, the two got together and had a blast with Lauren having a near-permanent grin on her face until the sun came up. Tammy and Lauren spent the rest of the weekend and subsequent weekends together for months. Lauren neglected her other friends who she quickly decided were boring in comparison with Tammy, who was a self-proclaimed wild child, who regularly trolled Tinder for casual sexual encounters, and was willing to try literally anything with anyone.

But months into the intense bonding, Lauren began to realize that all she and Tammy did was party and hang out at clubs. When she attempted to engage Tammy in deeper conversations about more substantive subject matters that were important to her, Tammy seemed to care less and would shift the discussions to something lighter.

In time, Lauren began to miss her other friends who enjoyed deeper conversational topics and more meaningful activities that didn't involve high school-type antics, many of whom she had known for several years and had stuck by her in good and bad times. She had been out of touch with most of her friends and had purposely shut out some as she and Tammy had been nearly exclusive in their friendship. When she reached out to the old friends she had cast aside, many had moved on and were not interested in re-engaging their friendship with Lauren. In less than a year, the relationship between Tammy and Lauren that had started so intensely had finally run its course.

**The Fun Committee** – These are the folks who are an absolute blast to be around, and if one is not careful, he or she can mistake a member of the fun committee for a committed friend with whom they can confide their deepest secrets and can grow to depend on the Fun Committee member in ways this type of friend is not equipped to handle.

Fun Committee members are the friends that you hang out with for a good time. The fun committee is usually made up of people that you party with, drink with, go to restaurants with, etc.

However, if you have a troubling or sensitive personal issue that you are struggling with, you might think twice before sharing it with a member of the 'fun committee, as they likely will not understand or be able to relate to you in the deep-serious light as they are used to seeing you in more fun and light-hearted scenarios.

### Pros of a Fun Committee Friend

One of the biggest indicators that you are in the midst of a 'Fun Committee' friendship is that most of your experiences with this person(s) involve casual social activities.

### Cons of a Fun Committee Friend

Fun Committee friends don't typically like to tackle serious subject matters or situations. They are there to have a good time and that is the main focus. If you are in a relationship with a 'Fun Committee' friend and you have a serious subject matter to discuss or a serious situation, you should consider involving a different type of friend.

### Signs of a Fun Committee Friend

Here are a few signs that you are dealing with a 'Fun Committee' friend:

Always involved with this individual in a social setting.

Drinking, laughing, and having a good time are your main interactions with this person.

Conversations with this individual are usually about something light and fun and not too deep.

### How to Best Deal with a Fun Committee Friend

It's pretty normal (and recommended) that you have at least a few of these types of friends in your life. If you are a serious person, having a balance of fun is necessary, as you can't always be serious and these types of friends can bring the levity and lightheartedness you need in your life.

### What if You are a Fun Committee Friend?

There is nothing wrong with having a good time. You just want to make sure you balance the fun with some depth and have the ability to be more serious when the situation calls for it.

# 8

—— · ——

## ACTIVITY PARTNER

*L* *loyd and Phillip met when Lloyd joined his church. Both men were retirees and were pleased to discover that they shared an interest in golf. Excited at the prospect of a new friend, Lloyd began inviting Phillip to play golf at local ranges. The men enjoyed the hours spent together.*

*One day, a neighbor dropped by Lloyd's house and introduced him to a multi-level marketing opportunity. Lloyd was thrilled about the idea of making a little supplemental income and signed up. Figuring that this was an excellent opportunity for Phillip as well, Lloyd shared the information about the business and enrolled his new friend.*

*However, it wasn't long before Lloyd discovered that when he attempted to engage Phillip in the new business that he was so excited about, Phillip was lackluster and disengaged. Attempts to motivate Phillip were unsuccessful.*

*When Lloyd invited Phillip to parties with other members of the new business, Phillip was withdrawn and did not interact with the other guests.*

*Lloyd began wondering what had happened to his friend who seemed so engaged when they were on the golf course but behaved like a completely different person outside of that element.*

An Activity Partner is a person you spend time with engaged in activities that you both find mutually satisfying. Examples of activities you and the Activity Partner might enjoy doing together could be pretty much anything such as skiing, wine tasting, engaging in crafts like scrapbooking, eating out at restaurants, going to the movies, or like Phillip and Lloyd, golfing.

To be perfectly honest, no one is at fault in the scenario between Phillip and Lloyd. They are solid friends within the context of their golf activities. The problem enters when Lloyd attempts to get Phillip to engage in a new activity outside of golf. Phillip is a solid friend, who is fully committed to Lloyd when it comes to their golfing activities. However, problems begin when Phillip is squeezed into a new activity that he likely does not find interesting.

Although similar to the Fun Committee member, a relationship with an Activity Partner is usually limited to a particular activity while Fun Committee members can bond over a variety of social activities. For the Activity Partner, the key to the relationship _is_ the activity. There is also the potential for the Activity Partner to be a bit deeper than the Fun Committee type of friend.

### Pros of an 'Activity Partner' Friend

The Activity Partner can be considered a "no frills" friendship because you usually know exactly what to expect with not a lot of extras. The great thing about having an Activity Partner is that you can expect structure around what you do.

### Cons of an "Activity Partner" Friend

This type of friend can be somewhat of a double-edged sword in that your interactions are often limited to the shared-in-common activity. Similar to Lloyd and Phillip, an Activity Partner might not do well in other settings outside of the activity or fit well into another role. For example, an Activity Partner might not be the right person with whom to discuss a challenge you're having at work, school, or in a romantic relationship. Depending on the depth of your relationship with an Activity Partner, it might be advisable to seek out someone else for support if you are going through something extreme.

### Signs of an 'Activity Partner' Friend

If you have a friend or two that fits into the Activity Partner category, especially if it is for more than one activity, then count yourself fortunate. Here are a few signs of Activity Partners:

- When you spend time with this individual, you are usually focused on a specific activity.

- You don't usually spend time with this person outside of your mutual activity.

- If you attempt to engage with this person in a different activity or role, it may not be well received.

### How to Best Deal with an Activity Partner Friend

I consider the Activity Partner to be a positive friend type and recommend that you have a person or two in your life that you can engage in specific activities that you both enjoy. In my experience, there is little worse than pressuring friends to engage in activities that they do not enjoy. I have a friend that doesn't like going to the movies or watching

TV but loves nature walks and hikes. For me to ask this friend to come with me to see the hottest new movie release is a guaranteed disappointment for both of us. However, if I ask this same person to go on a two-hour hike on a remote trail, I can be rest assured that she is going to show up ready and eager to go.

### What if You <u>are</u> an 'Activity Partner" Friend?

As mentioned previously, I consider the Activity Partner to be a positive friend type, and the only caution to be mindful of is that you do not become overly one-dimensional when it comes to the activity and that you be open to other interests.

# 9

## Foxhole Friend

$R$eggie started a new job as a senior associate at a well-respected law firm. While the firm had a reputation for being a great career launching pad, it was also known to be a grinding environment. As soon as Reggie started work, he quickly found himself putting in 70-80 hours a week on average. Earlier on, he met Jason, a junior associate, fresh out of an Ivy League law school. Right away, Reggie noticed Jason was struggling to keep up with his workload. He also wasn't getting along with his more senior colleagues and the partners often dumped an unduly amount of work on Jason and gave him a hard time. Reggie sympathized as he, too, was given an excessive amount of work and would often have run-ins with a few of the same partners.

One evening while both were staying late at the office, Reggie and Jason bonded over their work woes and found that they shared an interest in sports and had a mutual love of baseball. Their new found friendship was a refreshing oasis in an otherwise difficult work setting where both spent a lot of time pouring over contracts. Increasingly, Reggie and Jason spent time together outside of work and found they enjoyed each other's company.

One day, Reggie met a high school senior who was on his way to becoming a professional baseball player. The player's father hired Reggie to do some side work to help his son get signed with a major league team. Reggie negotiated a contract for the player that ended up being quite lucrative both for the player as well as for Reggie who collected a hefty commission. In a short period, more and more side work from professional and semi-pro athletes was offered. As a result, Reggie decided to leave the firm and strike out on his own to form a sports agency. Knowing Jason had a passion for the sports world, he invited his friend to join him in his newly formed business. Jason jumped at the chance.

During the first year, business was great but there were also challenges. Reggie began to understand why many of his former colleagues had been so hard on Jason. His work ethic left something to be desired and he seemed to not be nearly as engaged in the sports agency as he *had been at the law firm where he and Reggie had met. Still, Reggie and Jason made more money than they had at the firm. In year two, business became more challenging. Whereas, previous clients had come to them, the well had dried up and now Reggie and Jason had to actively look for new clients. While they were still able to make payroll and pay bills, the work was not as easily gained as it had been at first. Equally as disappointing, Reggie noticed that Jason did not seem as interested in the friendship as he had been previously. Reggie's attempts to get together with Jason for fun activities even to see a local AAA baseball game was met with resistance as Jason chose to spend time with his other friends. He declined Reggie's invitations and did not invite Reggie to spend time with him. Then without warning, Jason accepted a position in the legal department of a start-up company, left the sports agency, and never again attempted to contact Reggie.*

*Reggie felt hurt about the way Jason had left and had abandoned not only his position with the sports agency but their friendship.*

I've seen this scenario many times. You meet someone at work or school and you feel a genuine affinity for them, as if you two might be friends for life. It is especially painful when your work situation comes to an end or school lets out and the tight bond you shared with this person seemingly disappears as quickly as it had begun.

This is especially true if you are both thrown into a challenging or perilous situation where you feel like the two of you are taking on the world together. But as soon as the difficult situation comes to an end, your relationship with that person goes away.

This type of friendship that is born out of a challenging situation is what I call a 'Foxhole Friend.' The camaraderie you both feel can be made up of compassion for one another and a kindred spirit in light of the challenges you are both experiencing. These feelings often represent a genuine friendship, but in many instances, the friendship is only one of convenience. When you and your Foxhole Friend are no longer under the stressful situation that brought you together, you might find that you no longer hang out or even speak to each other the way that you used to or at all. It isn't that you had a fight or that you no longer like each other, it's just that the difficult situation that had bonded you together has come to an end and the bonding properties evaporate.

This is often the case with friendships that seemingly come and go, and is a natural process in many types of friendships. Not all friends are meant to remain with you for a lifetime; certain friends are seasonal. In other words, some friendships have an expiration date and are only meant to last for a set time. Once that set time expires, it's time to move on. This may not necessarily have anything to do with a particular conflict with a friend or an indiscretion such as a betrayal of some sort or a falling out, but could simply be that the friendship has run its course.

### Pros of a 'Foxhole' Friend

I consider a Foxhole Friend to be a positive relationship. The relationship only becomes not so positive when one of the Foxhole Friends is hoping to continue the relationship beyond the situation that brought the two together. If you recognize that the relationship you are in is a Foxhole Friend relationship and the crisis that brought you together is over, you understand that it is time to move on and are not hurt when the friend does not continue to reach out to you as he or she had done previously.

One of the greatest benefits of having a Foxhole Friend is that you have someone to commiserate with when you are going through the challenging situation and do not have to tough it out alone.

### Cons of a 'Foxhole' Friend

If you do not recognize the signs of a Foxhole Friend, you can be hurt when the relationship does not continue beyond the difficult situation that brought you together with your friend.

Years ago, I worked in a very intense environment that was hostile, to say the least. I befriended an executive assistant I will call "Gina," who supported the head of sales with whom I was a business partner. The executive had an abrasive personality and routinely lashed out at team members including Gina.

One day, the executive yelled at Gina in front of me and after he left, Gina began crying. From then on, she and I spent a lot of time together, commiserating about the executive until she eventually quit. After Gina left the company, she and I continued talking for several more months. When I finally left the company as well, Gina and I got together a few times and then the calls and texts became less and less frequent until Gina and I stopped talking altogether. There had not been any disagreement between us; our relationship had just run its course.

### Signs of a 'Foxhole' Friend

Here are a few signs that suggest you might be in a Foxhole Friend situation:

- You forge an intense friendship with a person for whom you are sharing a challenging situation at work, school, personal, etc.

- The intense relationship with this person came together as a result of your challenging situation.

- After you and your friend part from the situation that brought you together, it suddenly feels like you no longer have anything in common.

- When you reconnect with your friend, the closeness you once shared is no longer there and your time together feels weird for one or both of you.

### How to Deal with a 'Foxhole' Friend

Being aware of the type of friend you are dealing with is instrumental to you not being hurt when a relationship abruptly comes to an end, especially if you and your friend did not experience a fight or any other kind of fall out. Being in a relationship with a Foxhole Friend can be a bright spot in an otherwise difficult situation.

It is important to understand that when the crisis that you find yourselves in comes to an end, your friendship might end as well. Realizing that your friendship could go away when the trying situation comes to an end is the best way to deal with a Foxhole Friend.

### What if You <u>are</u> a "Foxhole" Friend?

There is nothing wrong with being a Foxhole Friend. There is a degree of pride in knowing that you were there for someone during one of the most difficult times that he or she could experience. The fact that you were there, providing a much-needed ear to listen, a shoulder to cry on, or comic relief is a good thing.

I believe there are times that perhaps, extending a Foxhole Friendship beyond the crisis could be a good thing.

If you find yourself in a Foxhole Friend relationship where the crisis that brought you and your friend together is about to come to an end, ask yourself if this might be a good relationship to continue beyond your situation. If the answer is yes, this is a good relationship to continue, then perhaps you should make an effort to maintain the relationship and help it grow.

But keep in mind that friendship is a two-way street. If the friend that was in the foxhole with you shows signs of not being interested in continuing your relationship after the challenging situation is over, recognize those signs, be respectful of your friend's decision, and be prepared to move on.

# 10

## HOLIDAY FRIEND

*A*aron was taking a vacation by himself. After a grueling semester of exams during his junior year of college, he found himself with a free week off and wanted to get away for a few days to relax. Since all of his friends had other plans and none were able to join him on a weeklong trip, Aaron decided to venture out on his own and take a 5-day Caribbean cruise.

It was a little uncomfortable that first day since most passengers were either a part of a family or were couples as he soon discovered when he was assigned to a regular table for meals.

But during that first chance encounter, Aaron met Ty, a guy the same age as Aaron, who was traveling with his dad and stepmom. The two guys hit it off instantly as they both shared similar tastes in music, sports, TV/movies, and celebrity crushes.

When Ty mentioned he wanted to go snorkeling the following day, Aaron was thrilled as he also wanted to snorkel and now had someone with whom to go. For the rest of the trip, Aaron and Ty were nearly inseparable and took advantage of all of the ship's amenities and recreational areas.

To Aaron's surprise, Ty was one of the coolest guys he had ever hung out with and he dreaded the trip coming to an end.

When the trip was finally over, the guys exchanged contact details and promised to stay in touch. Aaron was a bit disappointed when he learned that Ty lived across the country, but he was excited about possibly visiting him later in the year. As they went their separate ways, Aaron couldn't help but wonder if he had just met his new best buddy.

After the trip when Aaron returned home and was at his computer, he looked Ty up on Facebook and sent a friend request. When a few days had passed and there was no response to his request, he figured Ty and his parents were still traveling and were not home yet. Having recalled seeing Ty access Facebook from his smartphone several times during the cruise, the *explanation did not make sense. He tried texting Ty to say "Hey!" but his text message also went unanswered. He tried texting a few more times, but still, no reply.*

*After a few weeks went by with no communication from Ty, it became clear to Aaron that Ty was blowing him off, which really bummed him out as he wondered how he could have been so wrong about their friendship.*

I believe what Aaron and Ty experienced during that short vacation was indeed a genuine friendship. The problem occurred when Aaron assumed it was a lifelong friendship while Ty recognized that the friendship had an expiration date.

Personally, I enjoy Holiday friends and view them as good short-term friendships that are situational and typically focus on recreational situations. These friendships are usually made quickly and can feel as authentic as any long-term friendship you may have had.

Years ago, I found myself in a situation similar to Aaron's when I was vacationing with my aunt and met a married couple at the resort where we were staying. I hit it off with the wife and we had a blast during those 10 days. The wife felt like a close friend that I had known for years. We exchanged contact details when the trip was coming to an end but never reached out to one another.

The Holiday friend can also be experienced in situations that aren't vacation or holiday related.  When I was a teenager, my mom had a health crisis and was hospitalized for several days. During the hospital stay, my mom made friends with two of her roommates who all got along famously. They even exchanged information when my mom was being discharged to go home, but they never stayed in touch.

To my mom, the short-term relationships she had with her fellow roommates were priceless and made her unpleasant stay in the hospital feel more bearable.

The thing to remember about a Holiday friend is that this is a short-term friendship that will not last much longer than the situation that brought you two together. A Holiday friend is similar to a Foxhole friend, but the difference is that Foxhole friends are forged out of a difficult situation, whereas a Holiday friend is often made in much less stressful situations such as a vacation, a waiting room at the car dealership, or while standing in a long line at the store. A Holiday friendship is usually also a shorter term when compared with a Foxhole friendship which could last for years.

### Pros of a 'Holiday' Friend

The benefit of this type of friend is practically endless. These friendships start quickly and often feels as if the friendship started in the middle. People who engage in a Holiday friendship are often able to skip the awkwardness of slowly getting to know a person that many experience with other friendship types.

Holiday friends also tend to come at a time of need in one's life. The need does not have to be negative or dire but can be pleasant circumstances. As was the case between Aaron and Ty, both guys were in a comfortable environment where they did not have friends around them and were able to fulfill a mutual short-term need for companionship.

Other situations could be taking a new job and finding a temporary friendship with someone in another department that you regularly run into in the break room who shows instant friendship until you have time to meet others at the company and establish longer-term friendships. Another instance is perhaps, you're taking a trip and your flight is delayed for several hours. You strike up a conversation with another traveler and find that you really hit it off, but once you are ready to board the flight, the new friendship with your fellow traveler is over.

In 1989, I had just arrived home from school when the Loma Prieta earthquake struck the San Francisco Bay Area. Power and phone lines were knocked out in many areas throughout Northern California. I had several friends who lived blocks away from my house and since we couldn't use our phones to call out, I began walking to each friend's house to make sure they were okay. It had begun to get dark and I was a little scared to be walking in the pitch black without street lights, although there were more friends I still needed to check on.

A guy in a car pulled up next to me as I was walking and asked if I needed a ride. I took him up on his offer and he drove me to each house. Along the way, as we sat in impossibly heavy traffic, this guy and I had a great time getting to know one another and he seemed like an old friend I had just run into. About two hours later, I had checked on everyone and was ready to go home. The guy dropped me off in front of my house and I never saw him again. To this day, I cannot remember the guy's name, but I'll never forget my two-hour close friendship with him.

### Cons of a 'Holiday' Friend

Negative results only happen when a person attempts to hold onto a Holiday friend past the situation that brought about the short friendship. In the situation between Aaron and Ty, as long as the two were on the 5-day cruise, they were inseparable, but as soon as the cruise was over and the two went their separate ways, Ty had no more use for the relationship. The more Aaron reached out to Ty and was ignored, the more Aaron was disappointed even to the extent that he wondered if what he and Ty had shared was true friendship.

It is important to recognize when the situation bringing Holiday friends together is coming to an end, so you don't attempt to prolong the relationship against the will of the Holiday friend. I'm not suggesting that Aaron should have not attempted to stay in contact with Ty by sending a friend request on Facebook, but when Ty, who stayed in constant contact with other friends on Facebook during the cruise, ignored Aaron's friend requests, that should have been enough of a hint to Aaron that while the trip was fun and his time spent with Ty was awesome, their friendship was now over.

If you can recognize the end of a Holiday friendship, there really are no other negative sides of this friend type.

### Signs of a "Holiday" Friend

It's pretty easy to spot a Holiday friend. If you are in an unfamiliar situation that has an upcoming ending and gravitate towards someone with whom you share a mutual affection and an instant connection, you may have entered into a relationship with a Holiday friend.  One of the clearest signs that you are entering into a Holiday friendship is that the situation you are in is short-term. Here are a few other signs of a Holiday friendship:

- You find yourself gravitating towards a person while engaged in an unfamiliar situation.

- Your unfamiliar situation is one that is relatively short such as a vacation.

- When the situation where you met your friend comes to an end, he or she makes no attempt to remain in contact with you.

- If you reach out to your friend beyond the situation that brought you together, your attempts are either ignored or are coolly received.

### How to Deal with a 'Holiday' Friend

Dealing with a Holiday friend does not pose a challenge until the friendship either ends or shows signs of coming to an end. If the situation bringing two Holiday friends has a clear ending, then that's when dealing with this friendship type becomes something that both parties must face.

The one thing to remember if you are a Holiday friend, especially if you are the one that does not want to move forward in the friendship, is that you need to be sensitive to your soon-to-be former friend.

It should not be automatically assumed that just because you entered into a relationship that you believe is a Holiday friendship, the relationship must come to an end. If you and your friend clearly indicate that you would both like to continue the friendship beyond the situation that brought you together, then that is perfectly fine.

However, if the situation that brought you together comes to an end and either you or your friend backs away from the relationship, then it is time to accept that the relationship has reached its end point. The sooner you accept that your Holiday friendship has completed, the easier it is to open up to other new friends.

I'm not an advocate of prolonging a friendship just to be "nice" to the other person, but there is a right way to go about moving on from a short-term Holiday friendship.

The first approach should start subtle and if not received, you will have to be more direct. The way something is phrased can be encouraging or discouraging. Here are a few examples of subtly letting a person know that you are <u>not</u> interested in moving forward:

- *"It was really nice meeting you. Take care."*

- *"Good luck!"*

- *"I wish you the best."*

These phrases represent a way of saying "*goodbye*" without actually saying "goodbye."

Here are a few examples of subtly letting a person know that you <u>are</u> interested in moving forward:

- *"We should get together again soon!"*

- *"The next time we meet up we should..."*

- *"Are you interested in checking out...."*

Depending on your interest, with respect to your Holiday friend, you should attempt the subtle approach if you want to walk away from the friendship.

If your subtle hints of wanting to move on are ignored by your Holiday friend, the second-level approach to dealing with this person should include politely rejecting his or her invitations. If your Holiday friend still doesn't have a clue that you are not interested, then your next approach is simply doing what Ty did, by ignoring their invitations, texts, emails, phone calls, etc.

Completely ignoring should do the trick. If it does not, then you may have to directly confront and actually tell your Holiday friend that while the time spent with them was fun, it's time to call it quits. For most cases, the more subtle approaches will be all that's needed and the direct approach can be avoided altogether.

**What if You <u>are</u> a "Holiday" Friend?**

The last thing you should do when dealing with a Holiday friendship is to attempt to prolong the relationship especially if the other person is not interested. You will save yourself future heartache if you just accept that you had a wonderful friendship with a great person for a short season and move on.

# 11

━ ● ━

# HONORARY FRIEND

*A* mber and Rachel had been close friends since they met during their freshman year *of high school. During those first four years and all during college, the two regularly spoke on the phone and were excited about having careers and their own family. They were there for each other during life's major events including the birth of Amber's first child and Rachel's first marriage.*

*But as they grew older, Amber and Rachel's interests grew apart. After having her second child, Amber and her husband decided she would stop working and home-school the children. This meant they would have to move to an area where the cost of living was less expensive, meaning Amber would now be more than 2,000 miles away from Rachel.*

*After her first marriage failed, Rachel decided to put family life on hold and instead, she threw herself into work and became the successful career woman that she and Amber had both dreamed about becoming. She managed to climb the corporate ladder very quickly and was named a member of the executive staff of a large technology company.*

*When she received her big promotion to executive staff, Rachel was thrilled to share the news with her good friend, Amber. To Rachel's surprise, the conversation with Amber was stilted and uncomfortable. She thought her dearest friend would have been happy to hear her good news but during the conversation, there were uncomfortable silences and several interruptions when one of Amber's children or her husband needed something. Rachel decided not to read too much into Amber's lack of enthusiasm for her promotion.*

*Not long afterward, Rachel's company sent her on a business trip to visit a large customer that was in a city just 50 miles away from where Amber and her family had relocated. She decided to extend the trip for a few days so she could spend time with her friend.*

*The in-person visit with Amber proved to be as uncomfortable as the phone conversation had been when Rachel had shared the news of her promotion. During the visit, several of Amber's friends dropped by. All of her friends were stay-at-home moms and homeschoolers like Amber. They chatted about day-to-day subjects that were of no interest to Rachel. Private conversations with Amber were much the same. Amber talked non-stop about cute things the kids did or things happening in town. When Rachel talked about work, Amber's eyes glazed over and she seemed to tune out.*

*After the visit with Amber, Rachael came to the painful conclusion that the close friendship she had once shared with Amber had come to an end.*

The Honorary Friend is a person that you maintain a friendship with even though the dynamics of your relationship have changed dramatically.

It can be very painful for one or both parties of this type of friendship when you realize that the relationship has changed and is no longer the vibrant and comfortable place it had once been. It isn't necessary to assign blame to either friend; sometimes, people naturally grow apart.

In the example between Amber and Rachel, circumstances of life changed the friendship. When Amber and her husband decided that she would stop working so she could stay home and homeschool their children, she stopped being a career woman. This also meant that the dream of wildly successful careers that she and Rachel had previously shared was now changed for Amber, meaning that she and Rachel were now walking on separate paths and heading in different directions.

It is possible that Amber was responsible for purposely making the phone conversations and the in-person get together with Rachel so uncomfortable that Rachel would have no other choice but take the hint and move on. Given that the commonalities that they had once shared as ambitious young adults were no longer in effect for Amber, it is possible that she didn't know what to say to her friend.

It's also possible that the act of sacrificing her professional career to care for her family was made more apparent whenever she spoke with Rachel who was now living out their dream of a successful career and served as a reflection of what Amber's life could have been like had she remained in the workforce. Seeing Rachel successful may have been a painful reminder to Amber of the life she had sacrificed and the idea of this made her uncomfortable.

### Pros of an 'Honorary' Friend

The benefit of this friend type is that nothing actionable has happened that would suggest that you should officially end things with this friend. There, originally, were compelling reasons that you and the person who has become an Honorary friend had a strong friendship.

Unless this person commits a betrayal of some sort, there is no reason to take steps to end the friendship. And while you may have to adjust the way you spend time with this person, your friendship will have to evolve from close friends like what Amber and Rachel previously had to a lesser version of the friendship. In this case, the original close friendship becomes more of an 'honorary' friendship where you still care for your friend, but your time spent with this person will be much less frequent and might become more casual as time goes on.

### Cons of an 'Honorary' Friend

The worst part of an Honorary friendship is the pain you go through as you watch a relationship that had been vibrant unravel and shift into something that you no longer recognize. The disappointment of realizing that the qualities or circumstances that originally brought you and your friend together are no longer in effect is the negative side of this type of friendship. This negative side can be made worse if one or both of you decide to end the friendship, which may not necessarily be the right thing to do.

### Signs of an 'Honorary' Friend

The signs of this type of friendship are not too difficult to read. When you feel that there has been a change in either your life or your friend's life and you notice distance coming between you, something likely is happening. Here are a few signs that can suggest that your friendship may be shifting from what it had previously been to something more honorary:

- You notice that the time spent with this friend has dramatically decreased.

- When you do spend time with your friend, conversations feel forced and uncomfortable.

- Although you previously had a lot in common with this friend, he or she now feels like a stranger.

- You and your friend have developed friendships with other people that align better.

- The changes in your friendship with this person have caused you to wonder if it might be over between you two.

### How to Deal with an 'Honorary' Friend

I've mentioned this a few times, and it bears repeating - there is often a temptation for some people to want to formally end a friendship that is no longer thriving or let it die on its own. In certain instances, I believe this could be a mistake. If you and your friend had previously been close and had a quality relationship, but circumstances in your lives are changing the dynamics of your relationship and creating distance between you, then how you deal with your friend must change.

Let's say, for instance, you and your friend had been best friends and now you're noticing significant changes and the same interest level that had been there before has noticeably lessened. This doesn't mean the entire friendship is about to fold in on itself and you should pull away or cut it off, but it might just mean that you need to change the way you interact with this person, and rather than having an 'all or nothing' attitude, you can place this person who had previously been a 'best friend' into the 'Honorary friend' category. You will need to interact differently with this friend once she has been placed in this category, but at least, you will still be friends.

The best approach in dealing with the friend in question before concluding that your previously close friendship is now an Honorary friendship is to have a straight conversation that is free from accusations. You could begin by saying, "*I know we've both been really busy lately, but we should schedule time to catch up...*"

If your friend who used to always make time for you isn't doing that anymore, it can be hurtful. But keep in mind that there was a reason that you originally became close friends. If this person was worth it back then, he or she is still worth fighting for even if the friendship needs to be redefined.

Here are a few examples of what this redefinition might mean to the friendship:

- If you used to talk at least a few times a week and your friend has stopped initiating calling you, you can make it a point to call once a month.

- If you haven't heard from your close friend in several weeks, drop an email or text just to say "hello," and let your friend know you were thinking about her.

- If you and your friend previously shared intimate details with one another and she is now behaving more secretive or guarded, respect her privacy and don't pry (and try not to feel hurt).

Boundaries are key to successful friendships, especially a friendship that is experiencing a delicate phase where the two of you seem to be growing apart. Communication is key especially if you want to keep your friendship alive.

### What if You <u>are</u> an 'Honorary' Friend?

It can be hard to face that your close friendship with someone is transforming into something you no longer recognize. But some things, such as the direction that your friend's life is taking, is not something you can control.

If you have come to the conclusion that your friendship has changed and you have become an Honorary friend, you will need to come to terms with what the changes mean to your relationship.

Paths we walk on as friends often change and can veer off in opposite directions. This is not necessarily a good or a bad thing; it's just something that happens.

Being an Honorary friend may not be the type of friend you originally wanted with this person but it may be where you find yourself. Remember that you are still a friend and it is possible that life circumstances could cause your friendship to continue blossoming in an even better form.

# 12

## HIDDEN TREASURE

*A*n elderly man with a walker moved into the bottom-floor apartment across the way from where Alex lived with his mom and stepdad. One day, the elderly man, Mr. Waleed, stopped Alex as he was coming home from school and asked if he would help him move an easy chair in his living room.

The task was easy for Alex, who was on the junior varsity wrestling team at his high school. Afterward, Mr. Waleed invited Alex to sit down and have an afternoon tea with him.

Mr. Waleed was a widower who lived by himself in the apartment and Alex figured he was lonely for company and felt a bit sorry for him, so he agreed to stay for a while. Mr. Waleed poured two steaming cups of gold-colored tea that was minty and sweet that he explained was a popular drink back in Algeria where he was originally from.

Alex thought he would only stay for about 15 minutes, but ended up staying more than an hour as he was fascinated by Mr. Waleed's stories of travel and life experiences. When it was time for Alex to go home, Mr. Waleed invited him to come back again soon for a visit.

That Saturday, Alex dropped by Mr. Waleed's apartment to see if the elderly man needed any help. Mr. Waleed said he was fine, but invited Alex in. The two visited for several hours and this time, Mr. Waleed asked Alex about his life. Alex was amazed at how wise and helpful Mr. Waleed was when he confided in him about challenges he was having at school, with friends, and of course, with girls.

In time, Mr. Waleed didn't feel like a lonely old man whom he was being nice to but rather like a wise older friend with whom he enjoyed spending time, especially on Saturday mornings when Mr. Waleed would make strong Turkish coffee during their visits. One day, it dawned on Alex that out of all of his friends in school and the neighborhood, he was most comfortable with Mr. Waleed and thought of him as a best friend.

When wrestling season was in full gear, Alex had to attend extra practices at the school gym that took place every Saturday morning. When his buddies on the team would invite *him to have lunch or catch a movie after practices, Alex would pass so he could hurry back to Mr. Waleed's apartment to spend time with him instead. In time, Alex began to wonder if there was something wrong with him that he preferred to spend time with an elderly man over kids his age.*

The Hidden Treasure friend type often gets overlooked as a friend as he or she is not usually the obvious sort of person that one would look to for friendship. Hidden Treasure types are usually not members of the 'Fun Committee' or a typical 'Activity Partner.' However, the Hidden Treasure friend can be counted on to be loyal and dependable. In the example of Mr. Waleed and Alex, the man provided friendship in the form of hospitality, a listening ear, and wise advice to Alex. Given their significant age difference, a friendship between these two might not appear to be an obvious match, but for Alex, the friendship with Mr. Waleed proved to be a more genuine friendship than what he had experienced with people his age.

The Hidden Treasure friend type is not dependent on the age of the two friends. This friend type could be found in a workplace situation such as a supervisor finding a friendship with one of the administrative assistants or someone who works for the company next door. In a school situation, the Hidden Treasure friend might be the quiet, studious type that does not like to party befriending a partier or a jock, but this person would give you the shirt off their back if you needed it.

The challenge with the Hidden Treasure friendship is that those looking for a friend are typically looking for someone with whom they share a lot in common such as the same interests, coming from the same socioeconomic background, or sharing the same ethnicity. Often with a Hidden Treasure friend, opposites attract is the name of the game.

### Pros of a 'Hidden Treasure' Friend

A Hidden Treasure friendship is not usually proactively pursued as the two parties are usually polar opposites. This friend type usually makes his or her presence known when the person who is the object of friendship is in need. The obvious benefit of engaging with a Hidden Treasure friend is the genuine kindness, trustworthiness, and generosity this friend type offers.

### Cons of a 'Hidden Treasure' Friend

What makes this friend a 'Hidden Treasure' is that they do not naturally fit into what one would consider a friend mold. For example, looking at Mr. Waleed and Alex, no one would have paired them together as friends. Given the huge age gap between them and their differences in ethnicities, Mr. Waleed and Alex do not make an obvious match. Had

Mr. Waleed not asked Alex for his help in moving the living room chair or reached out to him in any other way, their paths would likely have never crossed.

In the case of a less enlightened or immature person, the stark differences with the Hidden Treasure friend could prove to be too much to handle and that immature individual could mistakenly walk away from what could prove to be a fruitful and satisfying relationship.

There are also outside influences that could be negative toward your relationship with a Hidden Treasure friend. In a situation like Mr. Waleed and Alex, it would not be surprising if Alex's parents or his friends expressed their concern about him spending so much time with an older gentleman with whom he has seemingly nothing in common.

### Signs of a 'Hidden Treasure' Friend

Unlike other friend types that might take a bit of analyzing to assess what you are dealing with; the Hidden Treasure friend type is fairly easy to spot. Here are a few signs that you might be dealing with a Hidden Treasure friend:

- The person is not immediately what you would consider to be your "friend type".

- Upon meeting this friend, you find that you really like him or her even if on the surface, you appear to have little in common with them.

- When you compare this person with your other friends, you don't see a natural fit.

- Your other friends comment about how odd it is that you are friends with this person and may give you a hard time about it.

- This friend who "isn't your type" proves to be kind and loyal towards you.

### How to Deal with a 'Hidden Treasure' Friend

The biggest threat to a Hidden Treasure friendship is outside influences such as other friends or "concerned" family members. The best way to deal with outsiders is for you and your Hidden Treasure friend to be comfortable with your relationship and decide that you are going to be friends. Depending on the relationship and what makes it a "Hidden Treasure," you may want to prepare polite responses for outsiders that voice a negative opinion about your friendship based on frivolous reasons. For example, if you are a professional in your late 20s and you happen to develop a close friendship with the elderly janitor at your job and you hang out with him for drinks, your coworkers in your peer group and friends might question your friendship. You may want to prepare a few polite, canned responses with your other friends such as, "He's really a great guy once you get to know him," or "Hey, the guy is cool, I like to mix it up!"

The bottom line is that if you have determined that you are dealing with a Hidden Treasure friend, you shouldn't worry about what others think about your friendship. Truthfully, unless you are in a situation where something inappropriate is going on or you are in danger, it isn't anyone's business.

**What if You <u>are</u> a 'Hidden Treasure' Friend?**

This is one of my favorite friend types and if you find yourself in the category of a "Hidden Treasure," then count yourself as privileged for possessing a high-quality character and being dependable.

The fact that you may be quite opposite in temperament, age, or have interests that are vastly different from your friend and yet, you two are still drawn together in a close bond speaks to the excellence that you bring to the relationship.

In many respects, you are an ideal friend and you should feel good about that. Don't change a thing.

# 13

## FULL-ON FRIEND

*L*isa and Olivia met during their sophomore year of high school when Lisa moved to the area with her mom following her parents' divorce. Both shared a mutual connection and quickly became friends. Olivia was an outgoing cheerleader who was quite popular whereas Lisa was introverted and very studious.

The differences in temperament complemented the friendship and at the end of the day, both Lisa and Olivia genuinely enjoyed each other. Lisa quickly acclimated to the new school by joining groups that interested her such as the chess club and the debate team, while Olivia busied herself with cheerleading and the drama club.

Oddly enough, Lisa and Olivia rarely spent time together while school was in session since their interests were so different. But since both Lisa and Olivia lived on the same block, they quickly created a habit of walking to and from school together. If Olivia was able to use her dad's car, she'd drive Lisa to school. The two would often spend hours together after school at one or the other's house doing homework. Sometimes, hours would pass as they studied together in comfortable silence. Occasionally, Olivia would sit on the bleachers in the gym doing homework waiting for Lisa as she finished up cheerleading practice so the two could walk home together. Weekends were usually spent in some activity sometimes with each other or with groups of other friends.

One weekend, Olivia dropped by Lisa's house unannounced when Lisa's mom was not home and caught Lisa in a compromising situation with a member of the chess team. While the sexual situation was embarrassing and caused nervous laughter, Olivia promised not to say anything to Lisa's mom or anyone at school.

To Lisa's pleasant surprise, no one at school commented or made on like they knew what had happened and Lisa's mom remained in the dark.

Prior to graduating from high school, Olivia was accepted to a local university and Lisa received a scholarship at a university across the country.

*Both stayed in contact throughout the school year and got together during breaks when both were home from university. Having made quality friendships over the years, Lisa and Olivia spent time with other friends as well as with each other. After completing her undergraduate degree, Olivia landed her first job in the town where she had attended high school with Olivia while Lisa took her first real job out of college in another state.*

*Within a few years of post-college adulthood, Lisa moved back to her hometown when Olivia informed her of a job at the same company where she worked. Lisa was immediately hired. The two spent the next five years at the company building their careers. Most people were aware they were friends, but Olivia and Lisa made close connections with other colleagues and managers.*

*Eventually, Lisa met a man, fell in love, and married. Olivia was the maid of honor at her wedding.*

While many may be under the assumption that in order to be close friends with someone, the two need to have nearly everything in common, must enjoy the same activities, come from the same backgrounds, and have the exact same temperaments. Lisa and Olivia, and many other Full-on Friends I know, prove this assumption as false.

Many Full-on Friends that I know don't necessarily speak to each other regularly, but when they do get together, it's as if they pick up where they left off; absent is the awkwardness of not knowing what to say or feeling uncomfortable in the other's presence.

I met the real "Lisa" and "Olivia" years ago. What struck me as most interesting about them was that not only were they very close but they were so confident in their friendship that both were comfortable taking on new friends. The jealousy and rivalry that I've often witnessed between close friends were totally absent with them.

Both Lisa and Olivia were also able to live separate lives and make decisions that were best for them without having to worry that the friendship would be compromised.

In terms of the other friend categories detailed in *The Friend Encyclopedia*, a Full-on Friend could easily fit into the Activity Partner and/or the Fun Committee category while at the same time displaying qualities of the Hidden Treasure. A person who is a Full-on Friend is the ideal friend to have and the type of friend to strive to become. A Full-on Friend is a person of integrity who keeps their word, is honest, and trustworthy and if their friend needs help in a time of need, a Full-on Friend would travel from one side of the earth to the other on their friend's behalf, at his or her own expense, and without hesitation, if that's what was called for.

**Pros of a 'Full-on' Friend**

Of all the friend types described in this book, the Full-on Friend is the type of friend I believe everyone should strive to have and to be. Full-on Friends are not easy to come by. Unfortunately, many people spend lifetimes having never encountered a Full-on Friend. It is my belief every person on the planet should endeavor to have at least one Full-on Friend in their life. The benefits of having a Full-on Friend are countless and can be summed up by saying you have a trustworthy person who is 100 percent in your corner when you have a Full-on Friend.

### Cons of a 'Full-on' Friend

Unlike the other friend descriptions detailed in *The Friend Encyclopedia*, there are absolutely no cons to having a Full-on Friend. These are positive individuals that add to your life and have your best interest at heart. These are people whom you enjoy and who enjoy you at both a surface level as well as a deep level. If I had my choice between having 100 good friends that were Fun Committee Members and Activity Partners versus only 4 Full-on Friends, I'd choose the 4 Full-on Friends every time.

### Signs of a 'Full-on' Friend

A few signs you can look for when evaluating a person for Full-on Friend consideration include the following:

- The friend you are considering demonstrates that they genuinely like you.

- In addition to liking you, this friend also enjoys you; they enjoy spending time with you and they proactively seek out opportunities to get together with you.

- This friend respects your thoughts and opinions and often takes your advice.

- When this friend makes a promise to you, he or she keeps it.

- The friend keeps your secrets confident and doesn't reveal them to others, no matter how juicy the secrets might be!

- This friend has your back and will still stand by you even when you're in the wrong.

- If someone were to speak ill of you, your friend would come to your defense.

- By no means would they talk against you or talk about you behind your back.

- If someone were to attack you, verbally or physically, your friend would come to your aid and fight on your behalf or alongside you and would not leave you hanging.

- This friend will challenge you when you are about to make a mistake.

### How to Deal with a 'Full-on' Friend

If you find yourself in the very fortunate position of having what you think might be a Full-on Friend, first of all, give thanks to all you consider holy that you have a person of this caliber in your life. You should treat this friendship as if it were a solid 24-karat bar of purest gold and make sure you are reciprocating the friendship. By reciprocating, I mean you are taking a look at the bullet points in the previous section and checking yourself against those bullets to make sure you are evenly matched with the person you think might be the Full-on Friend. For instance, make sure that you keep your friend's secrets and confidences, make sure you proactively spend time with him or her, keep the promises you make to your friend even if it is not convenient, and so forth.

Keep in mind some of the bullets listed in the Signs of a Full-on Friend section may not be everyday situations you'll find yourself in, but when challenging situations come up that involve you and your potential Full-on Friend, consider that time may be an opportunity to see if you or your would-be Full-on Friend can pass the Full-on Friend test.

### What if You <u>are</u> a "Full-on" Friend?

If you have evaluated the bullets in the Signs of the Full-on Friend section and have determined that you indeed have all the qualities of a Full-on Friend, then congratulate yourself; you have achieved what a very small minority of people have been able to accomplish. While it is good to strive to have more than one Full-on Friend in your inner circle, the idea of having 100 percent of your friendships to be Full-on Friends is not a realistic goal. Truthfully speaking, people with Full-on Friend qualities are not as numerous as other friend types and can be a challenge to come by.

Most people I know have a wide variety of the friend types detailed in *Friend Encyclopedia* and only one or two Full-on Friends. But if you are actively seeking new friends and are focusing on the Full-on Friend type, then keep the bullets listed in the Signs of the Full-on Friend section close by when evaluating others as potential Full-on Friends.

Being a Full-on Friend is an ongoing task and it's important to make sure you are living up to a high standard. I recommend reviewing those bullets frequently and that you proactively nurture those you consider to be potential Full-on Friends.

# 14

## YELLOW LIGHT FRIENDS

# 15

### — • —

# THE PRETENDER

*S*abrina had been close friends with Hailey since the two had first met in middle school. Both women had just graduated from college and had exciting career plans ahead of them. While Sabrina had landed an entry-level position at an advertising agency, Hailey decided to put her degree in education aside so she could pursue her dream of becoming a high fashion model in New York. Having been blessed with a beautiful face as well as long legs and a slender statuesque physique, Hailey was sure to make a big splash in the modeling world. Sabrina was convinced she would one day, soon, be a part of hiring her good friend Hailey for an ad campaign.

But soon after the move to New York, Hailey began calling Sabrina and asking to borrow money. New York was expensive and Hailey was having a hard time making ends meet between waiting tables at night and going on go-sees and auditions during the day. Sabrina was happy to help but wished Hailey paid back the money she had borrowed, which she rarely did.

One day, Hailey called Sabrina and excitedly told her she was in the final stages of signing a contract with a major fashion designer who had offered her an exclusive modeling gig for high-six-figures. According to Hailey, if she signed the contract, the designer would not allow her to take outside work and she would be committed to the exclusive deal for two years. She was not sure she wanted to be tied down that way when she was really hoping to build out a diverse modeling portfolio. However, she did say she was seriously considering the deal since she would be able to easily pay off her bills, could potentially buy an apartment in New York since she really liked it there, and more importantly, could pay Sabrina back for all the money she had borrowed. Sabrina was excited about the opportunity for Hailey.

But a few weeks later, Hailey called Sabrina to tell her she had decided against the exclusive deal with the designer at the last minute because she just didn't feel good about not being able to take on additional work, and while the decision might have seemed illogical, *she felt hopeful that she would now be open to taking on a variety of modeling gigs and build her portfolio faster than she would have, had she been exclusive with the designer.*

*Sabrina was disappointed and a little upset with Hailey but tried to be supportive. Not long after this, Hailey called again excited about an opportunity to play the lead in a film she had landed that had come up as a result of a screen test she had taken on a whim. The film was a thriller that was scheduled to be shot in Eastern Europe. Hailey said she would be paid handsomely and would be flying out immediately. She promised to get in touch with Sabrina as soon as she got situated with a mobile phone that could call out from Europe since her phone was strictly for use in the United States. Before hanging up, Hailey asked Sabrina for another loan, promising she would pay it back in a few weeks since she would be getting Screen Actor Guild wages and had to be paid at certain time intervals.*

*Sabrina wired money to Hailey in New York at once so she would have it in time for her trip to Europe and wished her luck. When over a month had passed and Sabrina had not heard from Hailey, she began to worry and called Hailey's mother to see if she had a mobile number or a way to reach Hailey in Europe.*

*To Sabrina's shock, Hailey's mother said that she did not know anything about a film shoot or a mobile number in Europe, but that Hailey was starting a new waitressing job at a restaurant in New York and she could call the restaurant before her shift started that evening.*

I've personally run into this "Pretenders" type of friend a few times in my life, and I'm always baffled by the lengths these people go to impress others. I find that these Pretenders are often deeply insecure and need to tell inflated and over-the-top stories about themselves to make the ones listening feel a little envious or at least believe that the Pretender is doing much better than they actually are.

At the heart of the matter, Pretenders cannot be trusted. One should be cautious about seriously considering a Pretender as a friend as it can never really be known what the Pretender's true intentions are.

### Pros of a 'Pretender' Friend

Pretenders tell great stories that can be exciting and very entertaining. The positive aspect about this friend is that they usually are fun to hang out with provided you have the understanding that you cannot believe a single word they say.

### Cons of a 'Pretender' Friend

The biggest negative about being friends with a pretender is that your relationship needs to be shallow and that you should be wary of sharing intimate details about your life with these individuals. A primary goal of a Pretender is to tell whoever will listen an outlandish story for the purpose of getting an emotional reaction from the listener, either jealousy or sympathy. A Pretender lies constantly making it nearly impossible to have a meaningful relationship based on trust.

### Signs of a "Pretender" Friend

Here are a few signs that indicate you might be dealing with a Pretender:

- The friend in question tells stories that are over-the-top outrageous that cannot be confirmed.

- Whenever you share something with this person, they always seemingly have to one-up you by sharing something bigger, better, or more outrageous than whatever you have shared.

- Rarely are you permitted into this person's world. For example, you aren't invited to his/her home, to meet their friends or have close dealings with them. You only get to hear about things through this person.

Many years ago, I was friends with a Pretender who told me an outrageous story about her dating a member of a well-known Rock band. I thought the story sounded too fantastic, and when I expressed an interest in meeting this rocker boyfriend, this friend who I will call "Julie" told me that wasn't possible. Over the months, Julie went on to tell me all kinds of new developments with this rocker including her wedding to him that I was not invited to attend and an alleged pregnancy that resulted in a miscarriage.

When I did my own sleuthing about this rocker "husband" of Julie's it turned out that he was happily married to a woman that was not Julie who had a different name and a radically different face! I never confronted my Pretender friend, Julie, about my discovery, but instead pulled back from our friendship.

### How to Deal with a 'Pretender' Friend

The best way to deal with this type of friend is at a distance. It is nearly impossible to have a meaningful relationship with this type of person since a quality relationship is based on truth and trust and neither of these qualities can be shared with a Pretender.

However, it is not necessary to end your association with a Pretender. Quite frankly, these people can be a blast to hang out with. Just bear in mind that you need to guard your privacy with these types of individuals and don't let them get too close.

### What if You are a 'Pretender' Friend?

The great thing about life is that you can make it into whatever you'd like it to be. If you find yourself constantly lying through your teeth about your accomplishments to impress people, you might be a Pretender, but this isn't the end of the world. At the heart of most Pretenders is insecurity that you are not good enough. If this describes you, then give yourself a break. Believe it or not, most people don't care that you aren't as wealthy as you say or that you don't make boss moves, or that whatever you are putting out there doesn't represent you.

When it comes to the Pretenders I've known in the past, I was never impressed with the outlandish stories they told me, including the ones Julie used to tell me. I was more interested in just having them as my friend. Truthfully, had they just been honest with me, I would have been cool with them and would have liked them just the same and maybe even more.

If you have relationships with individuals that you are lying to, please stop. If it makes sense to come clean to your friend that you have been lying, then do it. It's better that the friend hears from you about the lies you've been telling rather than catching you in one. In some cases, the friend might end your friendship, but not everyone will. To have quality friendships, it is important to be as honest as you can and to avoid lying, especially when it comes to lying about things that aren't that important enough to lie about.

# 16

## CHAMELEON

*J*aylyn and Camille met for the first time while standing in line at an organic juice bar. Camille initiated the conversation by complimenting Jaylyn on her workout suit. The two took a seat at the bar and chatted for well over an hour and discovered they had much in common including a love for running and hiking. They ended their conversation by exchanging contact details and agreed to hang out again.

The following weekend when Jaylyn met Camille in the parking lot next to a local trail for a run, Jaylyn was stunned to see that Camille was wearing the same workout suit she had complimented her on at the organic juice bar. The workout suit was even in the same deep purple color. Fortunately, Jaylyn had worn something different that day. Jaylyn thought it was a bit weird, but decided to ignore it and the two had an enjoyable run.

After that weekend, Jaylyn and Camille began hanging out regularly including spending time at each other's homes. Weeks after they had first met, Camille dropped by Jaylyn's place on a Saturday afternoon and asked her to come outside for a surprise.

Jaylyn was stunned at the sight of a new car Camille had just purchased, noting that the new car was the exact same make and model as hers. Thankfully, it was in a different color.

Jaylyn wanted to be happy for her friend's new car but felt the similarity was too close for comfort. She began wondering why Camille who seemed confident in so many ways would make such obvious copycat purchases.

The discomfort lessened as the two continued spending time together. Things between Jaylyn and Camille felt like they were getting back to normal. A few months after the new car incident, Camille invited Jaylyn and her boyfriend, Tim, over for a couples' dinner so Jaylyn could finally meet the mystery man Camille had been dating for a few weeks.

Jaylyn was not prepared for the biggest shock yet when she met the mystery man that evening. To Jaylyn's horror, the mystery man looked like he could have been Jaylyn's boyfriend, Tim's identical twin brother!

A Chameleon can be a male or female who does not have a healthy sense of self-esteem. These individuals are not comfortable with who they are and look externally at others that have favorable traits that they admire and attempt to emulate those traits. In some instances, the individual with the chameleon personality will just imitate a few traits like someone's laugh or mannerisms if they have a witty sense of humor or use their catch phrases that they find so amusing. In some instances, a chameleon will try to imitate the life of those they admire to the point of subversively attempting to overtake them.

In the story above, Camille imitating Jaylyn's clothing, car, and dating a guy that looked uncannily like Jaylyn's boyfriend, Tim, was undoubtedly unnerving for Jaylyn. However, Camille did not necessarily pose a threat. In many, if not most cases, chameleons are harmless individuals who imitate traits they admire in others out of their own insecurity. As the saying goes, imitation is the highest form of flattery.

**Pros of a 'Chameleon' Friend**

A Chameleon can be looked at as positively validating for the object of admiration. For the person viewed as admirable, this can be very affirming.

**Cons of a 'Chameleon' Friend**

As was in the case with Jaylyn and Camille, a Chameleon friend can take their desire to emulate the life of the individual they have engaged with to such a level that comes across as unnerving and creepy. If the imitation encroaches into the life of the one being imitated in an intrusive manner, the Chameleon may need to be confronted.

**Signs of a 'Chameleon' Friend**

Here are a few signs that can suggest you are dealing with a chameleon:

- You overhear the person delivering several of your signature sayings or catch phrases or those of others.

- The friend purchases several of the same items they have seen in your possession.

- The friend mimics you in countless areas in a manner that makes it clear they are shadowing you.

- In dating situations, the person often pursues the same individuals in which you have expressed interest or if you are already in a relationship with a significant other, they make inappropriate advances towards him or her.

**How to Deal with a 'Chameleon' Friend**

If you are to continue in a relationship with someone you have determined to be a Chameleon, it is important to assess to what extent your Chameleon friend is attempting to imitate you. If the imitation is limited to a few catchy phrases or admiring an item you own and going out and purchasing that same item, then they likely do not pose a serious threat.

However, if you notice your friend's obsession with imitating you crosses the admiration line into territories that are no longer appropriate or this person is taking measures to sabotage you in any way, then it is time to take action and put some distance between yourself and the Chameleon.

In this context, distance can range from limiting the time you spend with the Chameleon and avoiding sharing personal details with them. In extreme cases where this person could potentially harm you emotionally or physically, it's best to put distance between yourself and a Chameleon which might mean tacitly ending the friendship.

**What if You <u>are</u> a 'Chameleon' Friend?**

The interesting thing about Chameleons is that there are lots of them around. I believe every human being possesses some degree of Chameleon traits. I would even consider myself to have some traits of a Chameleon. For example, when I see something that I admire in someone such as a decoration in their home or an outfit they are wearing, I may go out and purchase the object for myself. However, my admiration stops there and does not include significant others or anything else that would be considered off-limits or something that would be inappropriate for me to pursue.

If after evaluating your behavior, you realize that your admiration of others crosses the line of what is appropriate, it is important to acknowledge that fact and make efforts to stop the inappropriate behavior. If stopping on your own proves challenging, then consider working with a behavior coach or therapist to help.

# 17

## AIR TRAFFIC CONTROLLER

*W*arren was thrilled to have met Mike, a cool guy in his early 30s who had just moved into the house across the street from where 18-year-old Warren lived with his parents. Mike owned a thriving auto repair shop and liked to fix up vintage cars at home. Mike seemingly had an answer to all of life's challenging questions. Whenever Warren brought up any subject matter, Mike would readily interject his opinion which was almost always in opposition to Warren's.

Mike's interjections were not just limited to topics that focused on cars but covered all aspects of Warren's life including his college major, part-time job, friends, and girls he was interested in. When it came to any girl Warren dated, Mike had an issue with her. The same was true for Warren's friends, all of whom Mike thought were losers. Whenever Warren introduced Mike to a new friend from college, Mike would attempt to discredit that person, telling Warren he should find better friends.

In time, Warren became very unsure of his own judgment and began involving Mike in his decision-making process, turning his friend into an oracle.

Upon graduating from college with a degree in mechanical engineering, Warren began interviewing at a variety of companies across the country and found out about a unique opportunity for a consulting gig with an automotive company for a substantial amount of money compared with what most recent college grads were able to land.

When he discussed the opportunity with Mike, the man suggested that he become Warren's "business partner" because he could coach him into thriving in the role and there could be partnerships that Warren could throw Mike's way that would benefit his auto repair business. He wrote up a contract that allotted himself 30 percent of all of Warren's future earnings as long as he worked in the automotive field. The contract was the first major red flag for Warren who was well aware that he would be doing almost all of the work and then handing over a third of the profit.

*Warren was not awarded the consulting gig but managed to find full-time work as a product engineer with a local medical device company. Warren's new boss was very accomplished and well-respected in the medical device design space. When Warren bragged to Mike about his new boss, Mike was quick to point out that no one was perfect including the new boss, whom Mike predicted would be a jerk. Whenever an opportunity presented itself, Mike went out of his way to put down Warren's boss.*

*In time, Warren grew weary of Mike's constant negativity, attempts to discredit others in his life, and questioning his every decision. He began putting distance between himself and Mike, stopped dropping by his house, and began ignoring his texts.*

*A year later, Warren received a call from an unfamiliar number on the display of his cell phone. He answered only to discover that the call was from Mike. It seemed Mike had gotten a new mobile number and wanted to make sure Warren had it. The two chatted and it wasn't long before Warren remembered some of Mike's nicer qualities that he had missed. Before he knew it, he and Mike were back to regularly hanging out again.*

*But the enjoyable reunion did not last long. Warren was in the midst of making a career change that he decided to discuss with Mike. As Warren stated his case for a career change into the aerospace industry, Mike cut him off and told Warren that he was brainless and incapable of making a quality decision. Warren was insulted and the two guys argued fiercely resulting in Mike punching Warren in the gut.*

*The unexpected violent outburst was the breaking point for Warren and he permanently ended his friendship with Mike that day.*

This example is quite extreme but happened to someone I know well. While most people who fall under the description of Air Traffic Controller (ATC) will not respond with violence as Mike did, these individuals can make the lives of their controlled friends miserable. The age difference in the example between Warren and Mike can also contribute to an ATC situation. A younger, more inexperienced friend in the relationship might look up to the older friend and feel a sense of gratitude that someone so much more experienced, knowledgeable, and worldly would take time with them.

These types of friends can be a handful to deal with. The challenging aspect of an ATC friend is that oftentimes, these people are truly well-meaning friends who just happen to have boundary issues and will often do or say things to friends that are inappropriate and sometimes hurtful. While it is not impossible to maintain a friendship with an ATC friend, it is absolutely necessary to set clear boundaries and at times, put distance between you and them.

**Pros of an 'Air Traffic Controller' Friend**

Most individuals would not seek friendship with someone if they did not possess positive qualities. A common positive trait of most ATCs is that they are deeply committed and caring friends. These individuals, for the most part, have good intentions toward their friends. In the story above between Warren and Mike, the draw of re-engaging in the friendship for Warren was the fact that Mike did have some nice qualities that he enjoyed. Unfortunately, the constant intrusion and overbearingness of Mike were equally a turn-off.

**Cons of an 'Air Traffic Controller' Friend**

The control aspect of ATCs is usually the biggest drawback of this type of relationship. In the case of Warren and Mike, it wasn't just that Mike always had input into the decisions Warren was considering, it was the fact that his input was so profoundly intrusive that Warren began doubting the quality of his own decisions. This is a common drawback when dealing with an ATC. Additionally, in many cases, ATCs will often slant their advice in such a way that it demonizes the opinions of others in the friend's life in such a way as to isolate the friend from others. As was the case with Warren and Mike, there can be a bullying aspect of an ATC that crosses the line of decency and puts the ATC friend into a negative influence that will need to be addressed.

**Signs of an 'Air Traffic Controller' Friend**

As was the case between Warren and Mike, often in an ATC situation, the controlling party can be significantly older than the one being controlled. In some instances, a younger person with a stronger personality can be the ATC. The biggest sign to look for if you think you might be dealing with an ATC is the control aspect of the relationship. Here are a few other signs that can suggest you might be dealing with an ATC:

- Your friend constantly questions the decisions you make.

- If you make a decision without your friend's input, they express their displeasure with you

- If you express an interest or admiration in others, your friend will point out something negative about the individual.

- You either notice an angry or a cooling attitude from your friend if you take advice from others.

**How to Deal with an 'Air Traffic Controller' Friend**

Managing a friendship with an ATC can be a bit tricky. As mentioned, one of the drawing factors of being friends with an ATC is they are often or, at least can be perceived as loyal and trustworthy friends. When dealing with someone who is a decent person, it can be a challenge to set strict boundaries or behave in a manner that might be perceived as unkind or disrespectful towards them. However, clear boundaries need to be set when dealing with this type of person. I want to put an emphasis on "clear" boundaries.

In the example of Warren and Mike, Warren had not established clear boundaries, so when Mike's advice became intrusive, Warren overreacted in an attempt to restore balance in his life. The overreaction resulted in Warren temporarily cutting Mike out of his life.

Had Warren established earlier that Mike was only permitted to provide advice when it was asked for or refused to listen when Mike bashed the opinions of others, he could have minimized Mike's meddling input early on and prevented the pent-up resentment in Mike that came as a result of being cut off.

**What if You are an "Air Traffic Controller" Friend?**

It's a good idea to review the bullets in the "Signs of an ATC" section and test the points in that section against yourself and how your friends respond to you. If after looking at that section you determine that you might have tendencies to be an ATC, it's important to be aware that when you feel an impulse to provide advice to your friend, you should consider refraining from giving it unless you are asked. The most important thing to be aware of is that you are not giving advice that has not been asked for by your friend.

Here are two techniques that might be of help to ensure you are not crossing your friend's boundary lines when it comes to providing intrusive input:

1. Only provide your input if your friend asks for it.

2. If the given situation your friend is in is something you feel compelled to provide input on, first ask your friend if he or she would like your input before you volunteer it.

Regarding the second technique, you should brace yourself that your friend might respond by saying that he or she does not want your input. While hearing a response like that from your friend might feel hurtful, you will know that you have just pushed against a boundary line that you cannot (or at least should not) cross. To prevent this from happening, the best course of action would be to not offer advice, just encourage your friend and tell them you are there for them should they need anything, and if they ask you for advice, only then do you provide it.

I find that oftentimes, a friend might talk about certain subjects or complain about things, not as an unspoken solicitation for advice, but rather just to vent and what they really want is someone to listen. For many, great comfort can come from having felt they were heard and understood by a good friend. They aren't necessarily looking for someone to help fix their situation.

You are very likely a caring person who really wants the best for your friend. While this is a great trait to have, make sure you temper those desires for wanting the best for your friend with what your friend wants and needs.

# 18

## THE LAYOVER

*V*anessa and Odelle had been friends for nearly 10 years. The two had met at a tradeshow where they worked for different competing companies. Most of their friends were married and Vanessa and Odelle were both single and in their late 30s. The two enjoyed reading books and catching the latest movies.

Then one day, a woman moved into the vacant house next door to where Vanessa lived. The new woman, Gretta, was in her early 30's, was new to the area, and was newly divorced. Vanessa suggested that she and Odelle hang out with Gretta to show her around and make her feel welcome.

At first, Odelle was reluctant but finally agreed to join Vanessa in hosting Gretta for dinner. Surprisingly, during the dinner, Gretta and Odelle hit it off and as the evening progressed, it didn't seem like Gretta cared much for Vanessa.

It wasn't long before Odelle and Gretta began spending time together and leaving Vanessa out of their activities. Vanessa felt left out and suggested that she, Vanessa, and Odelle hang out together. The few encounters she had with Odelle and Gretta together were unpleasant with Gretta behaving openly hostile towards her. To Vanessa's surprise, Odelle laughed at some of Gretta's mean-spirited cracks at her expense and didn't come to her aid. Not wanting to subject herself to Gretta's nastiness, Vanessa decided to distance herself from her next-door neighbor.

One day, to Vanessa's surprise, Odelle dropped by her house unexpectedly, explaining that Gretta was traveling for work and wanted to see if she wanted to hang out. Vanessa was still hurt by how Odelle had pretty much forsaken their friendship when Gretta showed up and how she had not come to her defense when Gretta was hostile toward her, but it didn't take long for her to forgive and forget. After having dinner with her old friend, Vanessa was thrilled that Odelle was back as she had missed spending time with her.

*However, a couple of weeks later, Gretta returned from her trip and Odelle was again missing in action as she went back to exclusively spending all of her free time with Gretta and ignoring Vanessa.*

I coined the term "Layover" friend to describe a person who is befriended by someone who does not view them as their preferred friend. However, one will remain in a friendship with a "Layover" person until they find other friends that they prefer and those preferred friends become their "Destination" friends. The person being used as a 'Layover' friend until someone better comes along is what I call a "Passenger" friend.

In our story example, Odelle was the Passenger friend, Gretta was Odelle's Destination friend as she was the type of friend that Odelle desired, and Vanessa was the 'Layover' friend that Odelle spent time with while he waited on her Destination friend, Gretta, to arrive.

In my opinion, the Layover friend is one of the most common friend types many people will encounter. In my own experience with friends, I think I've run into this friend type the most, in comparison to all the other friend types. It's pretty easy to understand how one could find him or herself involved in a Layover type of situation with a would-be friend.

Human beings are adaptable creatures and will often do things in not-so-ideal situations that they would likely not do in ideal situations. This applies to friendships. In our story with Vanessa and Odelle, the two women gravitated to one another as they were close in age and because most of their other friends were married and had other obligations. In a sense, the friendship between Vanessa and Odelle was born out of necessity. But when the newly divorced Gretta moved in next door to Vanessa, Gretta provided a new option for Odelle as she now had another single friend close to her age to spend time with that she preferred over Vanessa.

While Odelle could have handled the situation between Gretta and Vanessa in a more diplomatic and respectful way, her preference for the divorcee was neither right nor wrong; it was simply the way that she felt and she acted on those feelings.

Vanessa was the one who received the proverbial short end of the stick in this situation as she was the Layover friend who ended up with her feelings hurt when Odelle found her Destination friend whom she preferred and abruptly abandoned her friendship with Vanessa.

**Pros of a 'Layover' Friend**

The positive aspect of being in a Layover friendship is that during the time that you are in a friendship with your Passenger friend, things are usually going well and you are both having a decent time and in some cases, you are having a good time. With most Layover friendships, both parties have a need that the other is fulfilling in the time before the preferred Destination friend arrives. This is usually a positive experience and things don't usually go haywire until the Destination friend shows up.

In our story between Vanessa and Odelle, the two women had spent time together and enjoyed each other's company for years. The friendship between the two met their needs prior to Gretta moving in next door. When Gretta showed up, it quickly became obvious that Vanessa was Odelle's Layover friend and Odelle was ready to move on with her preferred Destination friend.

I have witnessed this type of friend in all stages of life from the very young to older adults. A friend of mine in her 30s, "Iris" complained to me about a new friend she had met at the gym. The new friend, "Sheri" had just moved to our area and didn't know anyone. Iris started spending time with Sheri hanging out at coffee shops, hiking, and going to the movies. She even brought Sheri over to my apartment one evening for dinner.

But a few months into the friendship, Iris was complaining that Sheri seemed to be disinterested in continuing a friendship with her as she had met people at work and had made other friends at the gym that she seemed to prefer over Iris. I understood right away that Iris had been Sheri's Layover friend until Sheri made the friends that she wanted. Once she had met other friends that she preferred more than Iris, Sheri moved on to her Destination friends.

### Cons of a 'Layover' Friend

The drawbacks of being in a friendship where you are the Layover are pretty clear. Once your Passenger friend finds Destination friends that he or she prefers over you, your Passenger friend moves on. When I say that your Passenger friend moves on, I don't necessarily mean that this friend disappears from your life entirely. If you had spent lots of time with this person before the Destination friends showed up, then you may only occasionally see your Passenger friend or the relationship that had previously been close may shift to something more casual.

The shift in the Layover relationship when the preferred Destination friend shows up is often disappointing and can be painful. A woman I know named Damaris was friends for several years with a woman named Lana and the two spent a lot of time together and were close until a mutual friend had a party and invited a client from her job named Jodie that really hit it off with Lana. In less than two months, Lana had all but ditched Damaris as she and Jodie pretty much became best friends.

For the person who is left behind like Damaris, the most negative part about being the Layover in a friendship is the feeling of abandonment, trying to figure out how to pick up the pieces, and wondering if you can trust another friend again.

**Signs of a "Layover" Friend**

The tricky part about being in a Layover friendship is that the signs often don't appear until after the Destination friend shows up and the damage begins. But occasionally, the signs can subtly reveal themselves prior to the arrival of a Destination friend. Here are a few signs that you may be in a Layover friendship:

- Your friend seems bored or dissatisfied when you hang out.

- When new people come onto the scene, your friend is eager to have them hang out with the two of you or will exclude you altogether from hanging out when he or she is with the new friend.

- Your friend's attitude towards you cools considerably when they meet new potential friends.

- If your friend's new potential friend is unkind to you, your friend does not come to your defense, or worse, he/she joins in on the unkindness.

With respect to the last bullet, if your friend shows disrespect towards you in terms of not defending you or even joining in on the attack when a new person comes onto the scene, you should seriously consider retreating from this person as that sort of disloyal behavior is unacceptable.

**How to Deal with a 'Layover' Friend**

If you find yourself in a situation with a person that you consider to be your Layover friend, how you manage the situation is important. Unless this person has done something unsavory to you and you were already looking for a reason to leave the friendship, there is no reason to ditch this friend or treat them poorly just because a new friend that you like better has entered your life.

Provided that your Layover friend is a good person and you just like the new friend better, you should consider ways of maintaining your friendship to some degree with the Layover friend rather than just abandoning them as you ride off into the sunset with your preferred Destination friend.

If you really would like to spend most of your time with the new Destination friend, there is nothing wrong with that, but you need to be mindful of the fact that before your Destination friend showed up, your Layover friend was spending time with you being loyal and meeting a friendship need in your life.

However, if there were problems in the friendship with the Layover friend, you may want to distance yourself but not abandon the friend altogether.

Think of your friends like gold coins and you had five 24-carat coins that were a little dull. Just because you found a treasure chest of shiny polished 24-carat gold coins, you wouldn't throw away the other not-so-shiny five coins because you know they still hold value.

If you can think of every good friendship as precious as a 24-carat gold coin, it will be a little tougher to simply cast aside a decent friend because you met someone else who makes you laugh more or you have more of a blast with when you hang out together.

If your Layover friend is a decent person but just not your preferred friend, here are a few ideas for how you could maintain a degree of friendship with this person without completely abandoning him or her and risk hurting their feelings or damaging your friendship:

- Invite your Layover friend to occasionally hang out with you and your Destination friend.

- Call or text your Layover friend just to say, "Hey!"

- Schedule one-on-one time with the Layover friend for something casual like coffee or lunch.

- If you have distanced yourself from your Layover friend, perhaps reach out and invite him or her to go for coffee or hiking.

One thing that I understand about a lot of people is that they don't like to be alone and will remain in a friendship with someone they don't really care for just so they aren't alone. In many cases, they will remain friends with someone whom they don't like until someone they do like comes along. For the Layover friend, that is the person that is not liked, when their Passenger friend finds someone they actually like and they leave the Layover friend, the abandonment can be devastating.

If you are in a situation where you are killing time with a Layover friend that you really don't like, you should evaluate your situation to assess if you should speak to your Layover friend and maybe fix the situation or if you should walk away from the relationship even before you find your Destination friends.

### What if You <u>are</u> a 'Layover' Friend?

I've been on both sides of the Layover Friend fence. Having been the Layover in my past, I know what it's like to be abandoned by someone I thought was my friend and the pain that comes from realizing that you are not the Destination friend. I also know the difficulty of dealing with a Layover friend when I have a Destination friend that I like better.

If you find yourself in the place of being a Layover friend, the key is not to dwell on why you were not the chosen Destination friend. Realize that you are still a worthwhile person and it may be that you did absolutely nothing wrong in the friendship but that your Passenger friend just found someone that they liked better.

Whatever you do, don't harass your Passenger friend about why they are not being as attentive in your friendship or demand that they tell you why they have chosen another person over you. If your Passenger friend has decided to move on with a Destination friend, then you need to accept their decision.

There is a saying, "*The heart wants what it wants.*" Oftentimes, when it comes to friendship, you can't find any compelling reasons why someone would walk away from a perfectly good friend in preference of someone else that may not be as awesome as you are, but it happens every day. If it has happened to you, don't spend too much time feeling bad about it, but be open to making your own new friends. Your new Destination friend is waiting for you!

# 19

## FAIR WEATHER FRIEND

*C*arol glanced at the clock for what seemed like the hundredth time that afternoon. Veronica was more than two hours late for Thanksgiving dinner. Carol and her new friend from work, Veronica, were in the same situation. Both had moved to a new town to start work at the same company and did not have enough money to fly home for the four-day weekend. The two young women had confirmed plans to spend the holiday together, but Veronica had not yet shown up.

Carol thought about calling Veronica's apartment again but hesitated. She had already called twice and had reached Veronica's roommate, Michelle, who had told her that Veronica was not there. The oven timer buzzed, signaling it was time to take out the turkey. The bird would need to rest for at least 30 minutes before carving. What the heck, she would swallow her pride and try to reach Veronica once more.

She dialed the number and the phone on the other end rang twice before a young woman picked up the phone.

"Hi, Michelle, this is Carol again. Did Veronica ever check in?"

The young woman paused. "Look Carol," Michelle began. "I'm going to be honest with you. I overheard Veronica on the phone earlier this morning accepting an invitation to Thanksgiving dinner with another friend who picked her up a few hours ago."

Carol's heart dropped. "What—"

"I was hoping Veronica would have had the decency to call you and tell you what was up or maybe invite you to the dinner, but obviously, she didn't...I'm sorry."

Ugly story isn't it? This actually happened to someone I knew many years ago. The girl in the story, Veronica, was someone with whom I was briefly acquainted and she had burned me in a much milder way than she had Carol. But when our mutual friend, Michelle, relayed this little story to me about Carol, I was truly stunned by the depth of

Veronica's selfishness, and more than a little grateful that my experience with Veronica had not been this egregious.

Unfortunately, there are plenty of Veronicas out there who view friendships in terms of what they can get out of it and usually go with the highest bidder. These types of friends think only of themselves and usually end up profoundly hurting the people who call them friends.

I'm not sure how they manage it, but most Fair Weather friends I've encountered seemingly have an unending supply of high-quality friends at their disposal. Even when they routinely disappoint these faithful friends, the Fair Weather friend always seems to land on their feet. Fair Weather friends are not necessarily bad people, but at the core of their being, they are selfish opportunists who take advantage of those around them including those they call friends.

### Pros of a 'Fair Weather' Friend

Fair Weather friends are often the proverbial "belle of the ball," whether they are male or female, many can be personable individuals who are loads of fun to be around. When the friendship weather is good and a Fair Weather friend is present, life can feel like a party. These individuals make great Fun Committee members because when fun is the order of the day, these types of friends will always show up ready to go.

### Cons of a 'Fair Weather' Friend

As was the case with Veronica and the unexpected invitation to Thanksgiving dinner from another friend, a Fair Weather friend will almost always opt for the more fun and exciting option or "better deal," regardless of what prior commitment they have made.

The impulse to always seek better is what drives the Fair Weather friend, and if a person who is on the receiving end of a Fair Weather friend is not careful, they will be let down when a "better deal" becomes available.

### Signs of a 'Fair Weather' Friend

A few signs that can suggest that you are dealing with a Fair Weather friend might include the following:

- You've scheduled an activity with your friend and he or she does not show up sometimes without giving you prior notice.

- You make plans with your friend and if another person shows up that your friend likes more than you, your original plans get scrapped.

- Your friend often breaks appointments at the last minute and usually has a flimsy or lame excuse.

- The strong friendship passion your friend demonstrates towards you seemingly dissipates when a new "shinier" person enters their life.

- Your friend always has a constant stream of "new friends" that enter and exit his or her life.

**How to Deal with a 'Fair Weather' Friend**

Strong boundaries are the order of the day when it comes to dealing with this type of friend. As mentioned, the desire to be around a Fair Weather friend often stems from the fact that these are usually fun individuals who are very personable and easy to get along with. But just because a person can be the life of the party and you enjoy their company does not mean you should permit them to treat you in a dismissive or disrespectful manner.

It is important to set the rules immediately with a Fair Weather friend. The first time this individual stands you up for a scheduled event or cancels at the last minute, you need to let them know that this type of behavior is not acceptable. This isn't to say that things don't come up. Obviously, things that are outside of our control happen. However, Fair Weather friends will bank on the fact that they can present their friend (you) with any flimsy excuse and it will be readily accepted.

If you notice a pattern of being stood up or cancelled that exceeds more than, say two or three times, then I strongly advise that you do not proactively schedule activities with this type of friend. If your suspected Fair Weather friend asks you why you don't want to schedule an activity with him or her, simply remind them that the last time you scheduled something, they flaked and that your time is too valuable to waste setting something up only for it to be dismissed.

If the Fair Weather friend truly values your friendship, they will think twice before standing you up for a "better deal."

**What if You _are_ a 'Fair Weather' Friend?**

If you've read through the Signs of a Fair Weather friend section and believe you may have some of those qualities, it is most important for you to be aware of the "better deal" tendency you might have when dealing with friends. A "better deal" is something great to strive for if you're at a car dealership or in a bartering situation. But there is no room for a "better deal" when it comes to your friends.

In the case of Carol and Veronica, when Veronica thought that she and Carol were in the same boat of being alone in a new town, far away from their respective families, and neither had the money to fly home for the holiday, the prospect of spending Thanksgiving day with Carol versus staying home alone was a "better deal."

But when another opportunity was presented to Veronica of having Thanksgiving dinner with another family and likely having an excellent meal versus what she and Carol would have prepared, it was a no-brainer for Veronica to take the "better deal" even if it meant abandoning Carol.

My general rule of thumb when it comes to dealing with friends is to simply keep my word. In other words, if I've promised my friend Jessica on Wednesday that we're going to hang out on Saturday afternoon, but my friend Sarah calls on Friday and wants to catch a movie on Saturday, I can do one of three things:

1. Juggle the schedule to accommodate both friends at different times on Saturday.

2. Ask Jessica if she's okay with Sarah tagging along with us and if she is not comfortable with that...

3. I ask Sarah for a rain check for hanging out and propose another day such as Sunday or the following weekend.

If I were a Fair Weather friend, however, and I preferred to hang out with Sarah instead of Jessica, one thing I would do is text Jessica on Saturday morning and pretend I had a headache, and then meet up with Sarah that afternoon. That would not be cool, especially if Sarah and I unexpectedly ran into Jessica at the movies!

The bottom line is if you believe you might have the qualities of a Fair Weather friend, you will need to constantly monitor yourself to make sure you are doing right by your friends by keeping your promises, and not sacrificing your friends for a "better deal."

# 20

— · —

# BF/GF Mind Controlled

*S*amantha and Heather had been good friends since the two met during their senior
year at university. Both accepted positions at the same company following graduation
and remained close. To Samantha, the friendship with Heather was nearly perfect except
when Heather met a guy. Whenever Heather was in a new relationship with a boyfriend,
Samantha would watch with disappointment as her good friend became a chameleon and
would adapt to whatever the new guy in her life was into, be it tastes in entertainment, food
and music choices, belief systems, and any other area one could imagine.

But the worst part of Heather taking on a new boyfriend meant that she would completely
abandon all friendships and would devote every waking moment to spending time with the
new guy. This meant she ignored all forms of communication including phone calls, texts,
and emails from anyone outside of the boyfriend, and would bail on plans she had with
Samantha and her other friends.

Early on, Samantha learned to accept Heather's all or nothing commitment when it came
to whatever guy was in her life. But as they entered their 30s, Heather's intense devotion to
boyfriends became wearisome. Whenever Samantha received a call from Heather after not
hearing from her for several months at a time, Samantha could predict with 100 percent
accuracy that Heather had just broken up with a guy or things were about to fall apart with
one. In time, Samantha decided to stop proactively pursuing a friendship with Heather.

After one particularly bad breakup, Heather got in touch with Samantha, apologized
for being so distant, and promised to take a break from dating for a while to focus on her
friendships and being a better person. To Samantha's surprise, the break lasted for well over
a year and during that time, Heather did not date and spent a significant amount of time
with Samantha doing fun activities like spa days and long talks or having dinner with
Samantha and Samantha's boyfriend, Cal. It was a good time for both ladies. Heather even
suggested that she and Samantha take a 10-day trip to Rio de Janeiro just for the two of

*them. It took more than a little convincing, but Samantha cleared the girls' only trip with Cal and the two women immediately bought tickets and started researching exciting points of interest in Rio.*

*Soon after their travel plans were finalized, an acquaintance of Heather's introduced her to a newly divorced guy. Heather and the new guy were instantly smitten and in less than a week they moved in together.*

*Samantha tried repeatedly to call Heather not knowing there was a new guy in her life and received voicemails and her calls were not returned. Feeling worried, Samantha dropped by Heather's townhouse unannounced and was greeted at the door by the new boyfriend.*

*Samantha instantly had a sinking feeling that the trip to Rio de Janeiro was about to be canceled. The trip was only a few weeks away and Heather had been unresponsive despite the many times Samantha had called and left voicemail messages asking about the trip. Finally, Heather broke the news to Samantha over voicemail that she had already canceled her reservation for the trip as she didn't want to be away from the new boyfriend, and she hoped Samantha would understand.*

For the "Samanthas" or the "Sams" out there, a friend like Heather can try one's patience. Over the years, beginning as early as middle school, I can recall being friends with a few "Heathers".

The BF/GF Mind Controlled friend is a man or woman who casts aside their other friends without care when a new love interest enters his or her life.

I'm not referring to the dynamic that should naturally change when a person meets a new romantic interest where they want to spend most of their free time with the new love. Of course, friends understand that when you have a new significant other in your life, the new relationship will become the dominant priority and you'll want to spend more time with the new sweetheart. However, when the regular pattern for you is that a new love interest becomes your sole purpose for breathing and as a result, your faithful friends become relics of the past that you completely dismiss until the romance begins to fade, then that's when problems begin.

### Pros of a 'BF/GF Mind Controlled' Friend

For the most part, these types of friends are nice people when they are not engaged in a romantic relationship. That's what makes their abandonment so troublesome for their friends. If the BF/GF Mind Controlled friend was a flakey friend, to begin with, then their disappearing act, when engaged in a new relationship, would not be an issue. In fact, you would probably be relieved when they had a new love interest to distract them so you wouldn't have to be bothered.

In our story with Samantha and Heather, the times in which Heather was not in a romantic relationship, Samantha considered her to be a solid friend.

### Cons of a 'BF/GF Mind Controlled' Friend

The cons of this type of friendship are obvious. The friends of this personality type feel abandoned the instant the BF/GF Mind Controlled friend becomes involved in a romance. The abandonment does not have to be as extreme as completely cutting off all communication with friends as was the case with Samantha and Heather.

Instantly adapting to the likes/dislikes of the romantic partner is also a con of this friend type. I once had a BF/GF Mind Controlled friend who behaved similarly when engaged in a romantic relationship. My friend, "Brianna" had adopted a vegan lifestyle to improve her health and had been successful with it for over two years when she met "Henry", a confirmed carnivore who hated vegetables. Instead of continuing her vegan lifestyle and preparing meat dishes that Henry liked, Brianna immediately began eating meat again and became physically ill after having been away from meat for so long. Oddly enough, she continued to eat meat and became even sicker.

### Signs of a 'BF/GF Mind Controlled' Friend

You might notice that the BF/GF Mind Controlled friend type has qualities that resemble a Fair Weather friend. However, a Fair Weather friend constantly looks for a "better deal" or a better opportunity and manages to take advantage of unsuspecting friends regardless of his or her romantic status. What separates a BF/GF Mind Controlled friend from a Fair Weather friend is that when the BF/GF Mind Controlled friend is not in a romantic relationship this friend type is usually loyal, engaging, and fun to be with. It is only when a BF/GF Mind Controlled friend becomes involved in a romantic relationship that their behavior can mimic that of a Fair Weather friend.

Here are a few signs that can suggest that you are dealing with a BF/GF Mind Controlled friend:

- Your friend will not make plans with you or other friends while in a romantic relationship.

- When you try to make plans with your friend, he or she will not agree to the plan unless the new love interest can come along.

- Your friend who just entered a new romantic relationship cancels plans that he/she made with you long before the new love interest came on the scene or they are simply a no-show.

- If your friend's new love interest does not care much for you, the friend distances him or herself or in extreme cases, will end the friendship.

**How to Deal with a 'BF/GF Mind Controlled' Friend**

How you deal with a BF/GF Mind Controlled friend depends solely on the depth of the friendship that you have with this person. As mentioned previously, if the person in question is a casual friend that you only occasionally spend time with for fun activities, then their disappearing acts while they're engaged in a romantic relationship is not a big deal.

However, if this person is a close friend, then it's important to talk to them about their past behavior with respect to romantic interests. You should be sensitive; it's best to have this discussion with your BF/GF Mind Controlled friend when they are not presently in a romantic relationship.

If you attempt to have this discussion while they are presently involved with a love interest or are in the middle of a breakup, you put yourself at risk of coming off as insensitive or offending your friend.

When the timing is better to have this straight talk with your BF/GF Mind Controlled friend, it's important that you emphasize to them how much you value them as a friend and want them in your life. You should also share with them that their past behavior of bailing out at the last minute on activities that you've planned so they can be with their romantic interest has disappointed you or has hurt your feelings.

Here are three things to remember when having this "tough talk" with your BF/GF Mind Controlled friend:

1. Make sure you are confronting your BF/GF Mind Controlled friend when they are <u>not</u> engaged in a romantic relationship or the middle of a breakup.

2. Make sure they know how much you value your friendship and look forward to spending time with them.

3. Set boundaries up front when scheduling an activity with a BF/GF Mind Controlled friend, stressing that canceling for a date with a new boyfriend or girlfriend is not acceptable if they have already confirmed an activity with you.

Adding to the third point above, if this person really values your friendship, they will respect the boundaries you have set and will keep their commitments to you regardless of their romantic status.

If, however, this person does not honor the boundary and breaks commitments they've made with you while engaged in a romantic relationship after you have spoken with them about this, you may want to put some distance between the two of you.

When they next attempt to engage in your friendship, it's important that you are upfront with them about their bad habit of breaking commitments with you when they are involved in a romantic relationship and how this behavior is not acceptable.

If the bad behavior continues, you will have to consider not making firm commitments with this individual and not allowing them to have access to your time until they show respect for it.

Bear in mind that BF/GF Mind Controlled friends have a common thread of a varying degree of insecurity. Emotionally healthy people who are comfortable with who they are and know their value do not fixate on every romantic interest to the exclusion of all other relationships.

While you want to make sure you set boundaries that prevent your BF/GF Mind Controlled friend from being disrespectful towards you in the relationship like Heather was to Samantha in our story, understanding how this person behaves when in a romantic relationship, you'll want to give this person their space.

**What if You are a 'BF/GF Mind Controlled' Friend?**

If after reading the Signs of a BF/GF Mind Controlled friend you see a few or more traits in yourself, recognize that you may have challenges to work through. It's possible that in the past you either knowingly or unknowingly neglected meaningful friendships while you were in a romantic relationship. If you are currently engaged in a romantic relationship, you should pay close attention to your present behavior.

If your friends truly mean something to you when you are not in a romantic relationship, then they should still retain their meaningfulness regardless of your romantic status.

Rather than second-guessing yourself, you might want to ask a few of your close friends if they feel that you become overly involved in your romantic relationships to the exclusion of your other friendships.

Be prepared for your friends potentially excusing your behavior because they care for you. But don't let yourself off the hook too easily if you believe that you may have been guilty in the past of BF/GF Mind Controlled behavior and have taken your friendships for granted.

To be honest, I believe most people have had at least one relationship in their lifetime that could qualify as a BF/GF Mind Controlled relationship, but when this sort of behavior becomes a regular pattern in your romantic relationships and poses problems with your friends, perhaps you should consider that this may be more problematic than you first thought.

If you have determined that you may be a BF/GF Mind Controlled friend, don't beat yourself up. Recognizing that you have at times been overly neglectful to your friends while you were romantically involved with a significant other is an important thing. Now you can make a conscious effort to improve.

Here are a few things you can do to show respect to your friends when you are involved in a romantic relationship:

- Designate a few days a month that you will spend time with your friends apart from your significant other and keep those commitments.

- If it is your habit to be in constant contact with your friends when you are not in a romantic relationship, make a point of sending a text or some form of communication a few times a week just to say hello when you are in a romantic relationship.

- Set calendar reminders on your computer or smartphone of important dates such as your friend's birthday or special anniversaries so you don't forget when you are in a romantic relationship. This would help you to not neglect your friends.

- Keep your word to your friends and don't break your commitments to get together.

These are just a few ideas for what you can do that might help you continue nurturing your friendships while you are in a romantic relationship.

Keep in mind that it is a blessing to have good friends just as it is a blessing to be a part of a romantic relationship. If you are fortunate enough to have both, make sure you don't take either for granted.

# 21

## GREEN-EYED MONSTER

*K*evin and Nate met for the first time at a party of a mutual friend. The two men hit it off instantly. Both worked in the field of accounting. Kevin owned and managed a small accounting firm and Nate had been out of work for several months, but was actively looking for full-time employment.

During a long philosophical discussion at a coffee house, Kevin confided in Nate that while his accounting firm had been thriving for the last year, the hours had been long and hard and he was considering hiring a subcontractor or two and might even consider taking on a partner. While he made no promises to Nate about a partnership, Kevin did say that he would consider his new friend for year-end projects that were sure to come in starting in October.

When the controller from a new start-up company contacted Kevin, he knew the three-month project the controller had in mind could help Nate dig out of his financial hole and would look good on his resume. He reached out to Nate with the offer and was caught off guard when Nate said he first wanted to discuss a partnership with Kevin's firm before considering the project. Nate told Kevin that he had worked hard over the course of his career and was owed a partnership without paying any of the proverbial dues as a sub-contractor since he had been an accountant longer than Kevin had and was more experienced.

Kevin was caught off guard by the demand. He wasn't comfortable with the idea of taking on a partner with so many entitlement issues, but he still felt bad for Nate's financial predicament with having been out of work for so long and he wanted to help his friend. Kevin told Nate he was still thinking about what direction his firm was headed in with respect to a partnership but for now, he could offer Nate a sub-contractor position for the project that would guarantee full-time wages for at least three months.

To Kevin's surprise, Nate refused the project, stating he needed to keep his time available for a regular full-time position and this project was not worth pursuing without a partner-

*ship. Nate's unexpected refusal to take the position put Kevin in a bind as he had already signed the contract with the controller at the start-up with the expectation that Nate would work the project and now he was obligated. Had he known that Nate would refuse, he would not have taken on the extra work as he was already at full capacity.*

*With the added responsibilities, Kevin put his energies into the new project and was relieved to not have time to spend with Nate.*

*Months had gone by before Nate finally reached out to Kevin to tell him the good news about the new regular full-time position he had just landed at a well-respected tech company that came with great benefits and excellent pay. Kevin was genuinely happy for Nate. To Kevin's surprise, Nate asked Kevin if he would serve as an accountability buddy to help keep him grounded. Kevin agreed.*

*It wasn't long before Nate began regularly calling Kevin with complaints about his new job and specifically about his boss, Elizabeth. To Kevin, Nate's complaints about his new boss were unfounded, sexist, and a little silly, but in the coming weeks, the near-daily calls with complaints about little incidents in the office were becoming wearisome.*

*Kevin reminded Nate that he had been out of work for a very long time, how Elizabeth had given him his big break, and that he should be grateful for the opportunity. One day, on his way home, Nate called Kevin to rant about a decision Elizabeth had made with which Nate did not agree. Kevin nearly wrecked his car when Nate boldly declared that Elizabeth was not fit to be the VP of Accounting and how Nate planned to set her up and take over her job.*

*Kevin was shaken by the admission and more than a little disgusted. He didn't sugarcoat his words to Nate about his declaration to take Elizabeth's job and the two men argued fiercely with Nate abruptly ending the call by hanging up on Kevin.*

*Kevin was relieved when Nate no longer called him. Several weeks later, Kevin was on LinkedIn when he saw a post from Nate stating that he was actively looking for a new job and seeking help from his connections.*

Maintaining a friendship with someone who has uncontrollable envy issues can be next to impossible. The problem with the Green-eyed Monster friend is that in many cases, the level of envy this friend operates in is rarely self-contained. In other words, the friend's envious feelings are not just something he or she can keep bottled up inside. Those feelings are usually hinted at in subtle and not-so-subtle ways that build upon until the friend says or acts in a manner that is hurtful towards you or others.

A few years ago, I took a close friend on an all-expense-paid international trip. This friend who I will call "Annie" was initially grateful, but as it drew closer to the time of the trip, Annie's attitude toward me began to cool. In the days leading up to the trip, Annie was short with me and demonstrated signs of disrespecting my boundaries.

When we were on the trip, Annie's treatment of me was hostile and she avoided me, ducking out on the tours I had prepaid for us. She also lashed out at others on the trip and was overall very unpleasant.

After the trip, I had a serious talk with Annie and she denied she had done anything wrong. Days after we had returned, I received a call from another mutual friend who shared with me that Annie had called him and told him unflattering things about me that he knew were lies. She even sent him a couple of emails that included an itemized list of accusations against me.

My feelings were hurt and I was floored by her behavior. I realized a reconciliation with Annie was not possible and I severed my relationship with her. As I reflected on my relationship with Annie, I made a few mistakes with her. I had received a promotion a few months earlier that included a hefty pay increase that I shared with Annie.

She commented that the money I was making was more than she and her husband had made with a combined income. It wasn't long after I had shared that information with Annie that I noticed her attitude toward me cooling. In hindsight, sharing my promotion and pay increase likely triggered envy in Annie and I should have kept those details to myself.

While it is not always recommended that you cut off ties with a friend that you know is envious like I eventually had to with Annie, it is important that you know what you are dealing with and avoid being blindsided by someone who carries a deep-seated resentment towards you and/or others for no other reason other than they have envy issues.

**Pros of a 'Green-eyed Monster' Friend**

Most Green-eyed Monsters I've encountered have been passionate people who have plenty of positive traits that draw others to them. For the most part, these individuals can be very personable and have a great sense of humor, unfortunately, making it at times effortless to become entangled with the Green-eyed Monster.

**Cons of a 'Green-eyed Monster' Friend**

As was the case with Nate and Kevin, Nate's Green-eyed Monster quickly emerged as the two became closer friends and manifested itself by Nate aggressively seeking a partnership in Kevin's accounting firm for which he had not yet proven himself worthy to receive. When Nate landed the position working with his new boss, Elizabeth, that envious trait did not take long to show up when he took issue with her in every situation, culminating with him making a play for his boss' job, which resulted in his dismissal.

The worst part of a Green-eyed Monster friend is that they spend an inordinate amount of time in their heads, pondering why someone has something they do not have and still feel entitled to it. Unfortunately, those thoughts can often lead to the Green-eyed Monster boldly crossing lines in significant ways such as Nate attempting to set up his boss to take her job. While it is not necessarily mandatory for one engaged in a relationship with a Green-eyed Monster to sever the relationship at the first sign of trouble, strong boundaries are an order with this type of friend.

**Signs of a 'Green-eyed Monster' Friend**

Listening to what this person says will likely be your first indicator that you might be dealing with a Green-eyed Monster. In the instance of Nate and Kevin, Nate demanding a partnership in Kevin's consultancy not long after meeting him should have set off alarms for Kevin. Sometimes, the signs that you are dealing with a Green-eyed Monster might be a bit more subtle. Here are a few signs that can suggest that you might be dealing with a Green-eyed Monster:

- The person frequently questions the degree to which others are qualified for the good things in their life.

- Constantly compares themselves with others who seem to be successful, have good lives, and/or be in good relationships.

- Regularly puts others down who seem to have a lot, and suggests that they don't deserve it.

- This person feels entitled to things that he or she has not earned.

- Assumes they are receiving the short end of the stick in most situations while another person in the same situation is undeserving.

**How to Deal with a 'Green-eyed Monster' Friend**

Once you determine you are dealing with a Green-eyed Monster, your next step is to evaluate the intentions of this friend. Boundaries are essential when dealing with Green-eyed Monsters so you need to decide exactly how far you will allow this person to pursue and go no further.

In the story of Kevin and Nate, Kevin did a great job of not caving into Nate's demand for a partnership especially when Nate refused to prove himself worthy of a partnership by rejecting the short-term consulting project. Had Kevin not had strong boundaries, he might have given in to Nate's demands and awarded him the partnership. Imagine how sorry Kevin would have been. Perhaps Nate would have sabotaged Kevin as he had planned to do with Elizabeth and kicked him out of his own firm!

Green-eyed Monsters can be persuasive when attempting to convince someone of something to which they feel entitled. To be able to successfully maintain a relationship with a Green-eyed Monster, you need to know just how far you will go with that person and determine to go no further. If the Green-eyed Monster crosses the line, you need to be ready to respond either with a strong rebuke or perhaps something more severe, even terminating the relationship if that becomes necessary.

In the instance between Kevin and Nate, Kevin chose to tacitly terminate his relationship after Nate hung up on him by not reaching out to him again.

**What if You are a 'Green-eyed Monster' Friend?**

If after reading the Signs of a Green-eyed Monster and you determine that you are a Green-eyed Monster, I applaud you for having the guts to be honest with yourself.

As stated previously, Green-eyed Monsters are often likable, passionate individuals who are often very personable. These are great qualities to have. The not-so-great part is the envious and entitled aspect of a Green-eyed Monster. The first step to overcoming these not-so-great qualities is to STOP comparing yourself with others. Realize that you are worthy, deserving, and okay without having to measure up to someone else and feel like you're lacking.

The second step is a bit tougher than the first and might feel as unnatural as putting your shoes on the opposite feet... but I want you to genuinely express happiness for people who receive good things, even if deep down inside, you wish it was you that had met a great significant other or who had gotten a promotion at work or who had just purchased a new house.

Sometimes, verbalizing your happiness for someone can actually materialize genuine feelings of joy for that person.

The third step is simply to restrain from saying or doing anything negative in response to someone's achievement that you feel should be yours or is something for which you think they are not qualified or deserving to receive.

Being a Green-eyed Monster is not the end of the world. If you recognize this quality in yourself and you set up your boundaries and determine not to allow the negative qualities to rule you, you can maintain control over the monster. If controlling these envious impulses is not something you think you can control on your own, a great option is reaching out to a licensed therapist or life coach who can give you a helping hand.

# 22

—— • ——

# FRIEND-IN-A-BOX

*M*elanie started her freshman year at a new high school where she didn't know anyone. One day, while walking home from school, Melanie met a girl she had seen a few times in the hallway. The girl, Shawna, was very friendly and definitely had the gift for gab. Unlike meeting someone for the first time where the conversation felt forced, talking with Shawna felt very natural and easy. To Melanie, it felt like Shawna was a long-lost friend whom she had known for years, and yet the reality was they had just met.

When Melanie reached her block where she lived with her parents, Shawna asked if she had to go home right away or if she could hang out for a while.

Pleased with the invitation to hang out, Melanie accepted Shawna's invitation and the two walked to a local coffee shop where they drank tea and chatted. The girls were having such a good time that Melanie didn't even notice that it was beginning to get dark. As she and Shawna walked home, Melanie wondered how she had not known that someone as cool as Shawna had lived just a block away.

From that day on, Melanie and Shawna were nearly inseparable. They walked to and from school and ate lunch together nearly every day. It went on like this for several weeks until one day, Shawna invited a new girl to join them for lunch named Wendy. At first, Melanie felt a little put off by Wendy's intrusion into the new world she had created with Shawna, but within a few lunches, Melanie warmed up to Wendy and enjoyed spending time with her as well as Shawna.

One day, Shawna did not show up for lunch, leaving Melanie and Wendy to eat together. It was a bit awkward without having Shawna there, but Melanie and Wendy quickly adjusted and became steady lunch buddies. It wasn't long before Melanie and Wendy observed Shawna hanging out with a new set of friends at lunch and completely leaving them out of the picture.

*Melanie was not sure what to make of Shawna's behavior but decided to widen her friendship net and meet other people. One day, Melanie's friend from middle school, Cheryl, reached out to Melanie to hang out one weekend. Melanie was thrilled to get together with Cheryl as the two had been close in middle school but because they now went to different high schools and lived far away from each other, they hadn't spent much time together.*

*During Cheryl's visit, Shawna, whom Melanie had not seen for a couple of weeks, dropped by unannounced to hang out. Melanie invited Shawna to spend time with her and Cheryl, believing they would all get along well.*

*During the visit, Melanie's mother asked her to help in the kitchen for a few minutes and when Melanie returned to the living room where she had left Cheryl and Shawna, the girls were gone. Melanie tried texting Shawna and her messages were not returned. When she texted Cheryl, Cheryl wrote back that she and Shawna had walked to Shawna's house and that she should join them there.*

*Melanie was offended by how Shawna, who had ignored her for weeks, then dropped by unannounced, had convinced one of Melanie's closest friends to come over to her house without saying anything.*

*By the time Melanie had arrived at Shawna's house, her anger had cooled a bit. Within minutes of arriving, Shawna began teasing Melanie about the acne on her cheeks and making other hurtful remarks at Melanie's expense.*

*Having not seen this side of Shawna and feeling ambushed, Melanie stood up to leave. Shawna called after her and said that she was only kidding.*

*Melanie ignored her and walked home. She had expected that Cheryl would soon follow after her, but she did not. Once home, Melanie sat alone in her room waiting for Cheryl to come back and stared at her phone waiting for a text from the girl she had considered to be one of her best friends, who also was supposed to stay over that night. To her deep disappointment, no text came and Cheryl never came back.*

I have heard variations of this type of story from several of the people I spoke with when questioned about what it was like for them in their teen years. Sadly, I've also heard variations of this type of scenario from those who have had their own "Friend-in-a-Box" experience as adults and realize this friend type is not limited to any particular age group. This friend type can be found at any stage of life.

It is quite easy to be taken in by a Friend-in-a-Box because of the deep level of trustworthiness these individuals can create almost instantly with people they meet. A

Friend-in-a-Box comes across as very open and approachable and often appears to be a sympathetic and understanding individual.

I have encountered several Friend-in-the-Box individuals in the workplace and find that they make excellent sales professionals. While this story featured Shawna as a Friend-in-a-Box with negative character traits, not all Friend-in-a-Box individuals necessarily have negative or backstabbing traits like Shawna. These friends can come in a variety of character types that vary from good to a not-so-good, and everything in between. A Friend-in-a-Box is different than the other friend types listed in *Friend Encyclopedia* in that they are usually a two-part friend type with the Friend-in-a-Box being the *ability* to easily allure would-be friends, but the actual friend type would be one of the remaining 26 friend types.

For example, in our story between Shawna and Melanie, Shawna is a Friend-in-a-Box whom Melanie soon discovers is also a Green-eyed Monster.

### Pros of a 'Friend-in-a-Box' Friend

As Melanie discovered, a Friend-in-a-Box has the gift of making the person opening the box feel as if they have just found their new best friend. Relationships with these types of individuals often begin lightning-fast and feel meaningful. When you consider how a typical friendship ordinarily begins, for example, you meet someone in a work, school, or social setting and they appear nice so you smile and say hello. Your interaction with that individual may not go beyond a friendly greeting for several weeks and then maybe the next step is having lunch in a group where the person you've greeted every morning is in attendance. During the group lunch, you have your first in-depth chat with that person and find that he or she seems nice.

From there, maybe you'll hang out again with the group and perhaps in a month or two, you might spend time with this person one-on-one, such as having coffee or lunch together.

Contrast this with a Friend-in-a-Box. The first day you meet the Friend-in-a-Box and say hello is likely also the first day you have lunch together.

If the Friend-in-a-Box has good character and their secondary type falls into a "green light" friend category, then jumping in with both feet in a relationship with this type of person can be mutually beneficial.

### Cons of a 'Friend-in-a-Box'

A Friend-in-a-Box has the uncanny ability to make you feel so at ease that you may let your guard down too quickly and reveal personal details about yourself too soon. If the

Friend-in-a-Box has a habit of gossiping about others, then the person revealing personal details could be providing fodder for this individual to share with others.

A Friend-in-a-Box can also make you feel as if they are your best friend. These feelings are not necessarily wrong, but if you are dealing with a Friend-in-a-Box that has a poor character like Shawna in our story, being quickly drawn into the charms of a Friend-in-a-Box can have serious drawbacks.

In the story with Melanie and Shawna, it is worth noting that Melanie's "good friend" Cheryl, was a prime example of someone taken in by Shawna's Friend-in-a-Box persuasive charms. While it is understandable how Cheryl would be so drawn to Shawna, Cheryl's behavior was not very friend-like. Melanie would be wise to think twice about considering Cheryl to be a close friend.

Most of the friend types in *Friend Encyclopedia* deal with the character of an individual, but a Friend-in-a-Box friend type is a bit different because it focuses more on the style of the friend type and not so much on the character. Frankly, a Friend-in-a-Box friend is a mystery that has to be uncovered on a case-by-case basis.

Once you know that you are dealing with a Friend-in-a-Box (and you should know pretty quickly), you should begin assessing the Friend-in-a-Box's trustworthiness before revealing personal information or getting too close with this individual.

**Signs of a 'Friend-in-a-Box'**

When dealing with a Friend-in-a-Box, it's important to slow down and carefully observe the character of this person. Just having the gift of talking to anyone and behaving in a friendly manner is not a qualifier for a meaningful friendship. Just like any other person you would be friends with, you need to scrutinize a Friend-in-a-Box as well. Here are a few signs that might suggest that you are encountering a Friend-in-a-Box:

- Upon meeting this person, you feel a near-instant emotional connection and feel at ease in their presence.

- They exude a feeling of trustworthiness almost immediately.

- Engaging with this person makes you want to open up and share your confidences and secrets.

- You have the desire to be close friends with this individual fairly quickly.

**How to Deal with a 'Friend-in-a-Box'**

The challenging part about dealing with a Friend-in-a-Box is uncovering the true character type that goes beyond the outer shell of their friendliness.

As mentioned previously, a Friend-in-a-Box always comes in two parts – the alluring Friend-in-a-Box part and the second part which is the true category, which could be a positive, neutral, or negative type. Here are five examples of a Friend-in-a-Box that I've encountered in my lifetime and the second part the individuals revealed.

1. Friend-in-a-Box #1 – Met in elementary school and after a while, her secondary part was revealed to be a *Vampire*.

2. Friend-in-a-Box #2 – Met in high school and after a while, her secondary part was revealed as *The Judas*.

3. Friend-in-a-Box #3 – Met in college and after a while, her secondary part was revealed as a *Full-on Friend*.

4. Friend-in-a-Box #4 – Met at work and after a while, her secondary part was revealed as an *Activity Partner*.

5. Friend-in-a-Box #5 – Met when I moved into a new apartment and after a while, her secondary part was revealed as a *Fun Committee Member*.

Many people are so taken in by the outer friendliness of a Friend-in-a-Box that they overlook that very important secondary friend type part and proceed as if they are dealing with a faithful and trustworthy individual when the reality is that this person has not been properly vetted.

When dealing with a Friend-in-a-Box, it's important that you realize that while you are encountering someone who is friendly, personable, and perhaps persuasive, that is only the outer shell. The challenge lies in not acting on your own emotions when it comes to a Friend-in-a-Box but behaving as you would with an ordinary person you were befriending and vetting their character before sharing confidences and giving access to your personal details.

### What if You <u>are</u> a 'Friend-in-a-Box'?

If you've read through the above description and see yourself as this Friend-in-a-Box, consider yourself fortunate to have the ability to influence others. Your challenge will be making sure your character is healthy and strong to ensure that what is inside your box is positive and mutually beneficial to yourself and others. If you're looking for suggestions to help build healthy character, take a look at the *Friend Encyclopedia* chapter on a "Good FFIT".

# 23

# TABLE TURNER

*A*ndrew and Seth met during their teen years. Seth lived with his grandparents while Andrew had just moved in with a foster family that lived across the street from Seth's grandparents.

The boys experienced an instant connection the day they met when Andrew was placed in the home by a social worker. When Andrew turned 18 and was required to move out of his foster home. Seth decided to move in with his friend, and the two rented an apartment across town.

Having bounced around from more than 15 foster homes, Andrew carried a lot of emotional and relationship baggage. Seth was emotionally stronger by far and was a constant source of encouragement to Andrew as the young man adjusted to work environments and dealt with questionable girlfriends, some of whom played head games and mistreated him.

In time, Andrew decided to enroll in college, and through hard work and lots of pep talk sessions with Seth, he managed to finish his degree and take on his first professional job. While the first job out of college was not what he had hoped for, Andrew managed to tough it out there for two years before landing a very lucrative job where his responsibilities significantly increased along with his pay.

Andrew was excited about the wonderful turn of events in his life that included not only his promotion on his job but a corporate lawyer girlfriend whom he had begun dating. However, he noticed that his relationship with Seth had begun to cool.

Seth had opted to skip college to work full-time and had secured a job working for the city in which he and Andrew lived that paid well and had great benefits. Even though he and Andrew had both worked full-time right out of high school, Seth had always earned significantly more money than his friend.

But Andrew's college degree and promotion turned the tables on him; he now made significantly more than Seth.

*Additionally, Seth had a steady girlfriend he had met right after he and Andrew had graduated from high school. While Seth and his girlfriend had been together for several years, the girlfriend, Lexie, had recently broken up with Seth and started seeing a new guy who owned his own business and several homes.*

*Andrew shared with Seth the happy news that he had proposed marriage to his corporate lawyer girlfriend and they were now engaged. He asked his longtime friend to serve as the best man at his wedding. Seth verbalized his happiness for Andrew and agreed to be the best man, but Andrew sensed that something was not right.*

*On the wedding day, Seth was a no-show.*

When a friendship dynamic starts out with one person being emotionally stronger and more accomplished than the other, it can complement the overall relationship and work well. However, if during the friendship, the dynamic shifts and the one that was the emotional weaker and less accomplished gains strength and becomes emotionally stronger and more accomplished, then the relationship can suffer.

Many friendships can start well and continue successfully for several years until one of the friends makes improvements that can include anything from making a professional gain to finding love with a new significant other, and just about any other forward moving endeavor one can imagine.

Often, what makes a Table Turner friendship work is that the dynamic is based on one friend being weaker than the other. This is sometimes compounded by the weaker friend having a degree of dependence on the stronger friend which can be a source of comfort for both. As long as the original dynamic remains the same –the weaker depending on the stronger—the friendship can remain solid for however as long as that dynamic remains. But if the weaker manages to overcome the weakness and becomes strong, then the dynamic changes and this can cause the friendship to become unstable.

**Pros of a 'Table Turner' Friend**

The great aspect of a Table Turner friend is that this person is generally a good friend who has demonstrated loyalty and dependability. This type of friend is often someone that you may consider to be as close as a brother or sister. Before the shift occurs and the weaker becomes stronger, the friendship with this person can be something that you can see lasting long into the future, and maybe, even a lifetime.

**Cons of a 'Table Turner' Friend**

The negative side of this friend type doesn't reveal itself until the weaker friend becomes stronger. In the case of Andrew and Seth, the relationship between the two could be compared with brothers. They were always there for one another and encouraged each other in good and bad times.

Andrew had always been the more emotionally dependent friend who made bad decisions when it came to girlfriends and struggled at first in his career. But when he began to elevate based on his maturing and making better overall life decisions, the friendship dynamic between him and Seth began to shift.

When Andrew completed his college degree (Seth skipped college and jumped right into the workforce), received a promotion on his job that caused his salary to exceed Seth's and he also became engaged to a corporate attorney, the dramatic shift greatly upset the balance of their friendship and was too much for Seth to bear, especially given the fact that Seth's long-term girlfriend leveled up with a new man who was significantly more accomplished than Seth.

Imagine for a moment that the tables had not turned and Seth was the one who blossomed in his career, went to night school, finished his degree, met an awesome woman, and became engaged, the friendship dynamic would have been unchanged and Seth and Andrew would have likely remained friends.

It was only when the weaker friend became stronger that the friendship became unbalanced.

### Signs of a 'Table Turner' Friend

The maturity and character of the stronger friend will determine how much the tables will turn in a Table Turner friendship. For example, if the stronger friend is somewhat immature, the tables can turn dramatically and end in a harmful manner as was the case for Andrew when his closest friend and best man, Seth, was a no-show at his wedding.

In a worst-case scenario, if the Table Turner friend is immature and lacks character, the table can turn so far that it can end in a betrayal.

In the 1992 film, Malcolm X, that starred Denzel Washington, there was a storyline of Malcolm X when he was in prison and became friends with a fellow inmate named Brother Baines. Baines was responsible for mentoring Malcolm and teaching him about Islam. During the incarceration of the two, Malcolm sat at Brother Baines' feet and learned about himself and his place in Islam. When Malcolm was released from prison, he joined Brother Baines who had already been released, and continued being mentored by him and others in the Nation of Islam.

Being a natural-born leader, it didn't take long for Malcolm to quickly move up the ranks in Islam and surpass Brother Baines ranking as Malcolm became the face and mouthpiece of Islam. Rather than being happy for his friend who he had helped nurture from being a petty criminal to a worldwide influencer, Brother Baines became envious and began working against Malcolm. It is alleged that Brother Baines may have been one of the insiders that helped facilitate Malcolm's assassination.

I was stunned to watch a Table Turner situation play out on the big screen, and it was a reminder to me that if unchecked, a Table Turner friendship can turn deadly.

If you have always been the weaker one in the friendship, but find yourself maturing, getting emotionally stronger, and achieving tangible results, it is important to observe any changes in your friendship and attempt to get in front of them before they negatively affect you and your friend.

Here are a few signs that can suggest that a problem might be brewing and your friend is in danger of becoming a Table Turner friend:

- Your friend appears to be distancing himself from you.

- As you begin to level up in life, there is a noticeable cooling of your friendship when nothing in particular has happened (no fight or argument between you and your friend).

- Your friend suddenly stops calling, texting, or emailing you and does not return your calls, texts, or emails.

- When you ask your friend if something is wrong, he/she says everything is fine.

**How to Deal with a 'Table Turner' Friend**

Being sensitive to the needs of your Table Turner friend is the first step in dealing with this friend type. If you have always been the weaker one in the friendship, you should be mindful of your newfound strength, promotion, or success and be careful that you don't flaunt it in your friend's face. It's not that you should have to veil, pretend, or overlook your successes, but there's a difference between simply walking in your new success and showing off or parading your achievements. Here are three examples of your new strength and ways you could downplay it a little in order to be sensitive to your Table Turner friend:

Example #1 – Both you and your friend have always been overweight, but you decided to do something about it and you lose the excess pounds. You are now at a healthy weight and you look great, but your friend is still overweight. When you are around your friend, you should avoid wearing revealing clothing or bragging about your weight loss and all the attention you're getting now.

Example #2 – You and your friend are in the same profession, but your friend has always been savvier in the workplace and he just completed his master's degree in business. But oddly enough, you are the one who lands a new job that is more senior than what your friend currently holds and your pay is significantly more than your friend's. Make it a point to not discuss your new salary that you know is significantly more than theirs and avoid long discussions about your position.

Example #3 – Your friend has always had a girlfriend and you have been single almost the entire time of your friendship. Just as you finally get a girlfriend, your friend's relationship with his significant other comes to an abrupt end. Avoid talking about how wonderful your new girlfriend is and purposely schedule some one-on-one time with your friend.

The above examples are not about you coddling your friend and hiding your good fortune, but to keep it real it isn't necessary to flaunt and show off, especially when your close friend might be experiencing a downturn. Above all, keeping the lines of communication open is key when you are experiencing a shift in the friendship dynamic where the weaker friend is becoming stronger, healthier, or more successful. It is human nature to feel a little threatened when the dynamic changes in a friendship.

If you are sensitive to the changes and make a few minor adjustments, you may be able to avoid a Table Turner situation from happening or escalating into something more severe such as your friend behaving out of character in a way that could be hurtful towards you or destroy your relationship.

Typically, the Table Turner type of friend can be harmless in terms of the weaker friend that becomes strong. But in extreme cases of the stronger friend becoming weaker, this friend can completely disengage from the friendship and in worst case scenarios, the Table Turner friend can completely turn on the other friend and betray them. If you are the formerly weaker friend that has become strong and more successful and you notice any of the signs that your friend might be becoming a Table Turner, you should be on high alert for changes in your friend's character and act accordingly.

**What if You are a 'Table Turner' Friend?**

Intellectually, we all know that seeing that friend who has struggled in a certain area overcome that weakness and become strong should bring us joy, but emotionally, that doesn't always happen.

If you are the one in the relationship that has always been the stronger or more successful one, it can feel like a punch in the gut when you see your weaker friend coming into his or her own and becoming strong or finding success on their own, especially if they had previously leaned on you for support and are no longer doing this. Your friend's new independence can make you feel unneeded or unwanted and this can upset the dynamic of your friendship.

Nonetheless, if you truly care about your friend, then you should be happy that she/he has matured and is becoming stronger. Here are a few ways that can help you adjust to the new dynamic change in the friendship:

**Give your friend space and allow yourself space as well** – This does not mean that you should purposely avoid your friend, but if your friend indicates that she needs space, then provide it. This applies to you as well if you need a little space for a short time as you adjust to the new dynamic.

**Tell your friend how proud you are of their positive changes** – Saying this might make you bristle at first and feel a bit unnatural, but your friend will love hearing it and it might make you feel better after having said it.

**Be proactive in giving your friend your approval** – Regardless of your friend's new strength and status, she is still your friend and should respect your opinion. Go out of your way to express that you like the new positive changes he/she has made.

**Refrain from giving advice unless asked** – If your friend was the type that relied on your advice before making a decision, this behavior may change as she grows in confidence. Make it a point to not offer advice unless asked.

Part of being a good friend includes sacrifice. If you think you may have Table Turner tendencies but still care about your friendship with your friend who is experiencing the positive changes, then for a little while, you will have to put aside your feelings to be able to adjust to the dynamic change in your relationship so you can enter the next growth phase of your friendship. In time, you will hopefully be able to work through the uncomfortable feelings and settle back into a comfortable friendship in which you will both be stronger.

# 24

## RED LIGHT FRIENDS

# 25

## PARASITE

*Ted was an aspiring musician who was a keyboardist and lead singer in an up-and-coming band. While waiting for his big break, Ted worked as an assistant manager of a local record store where he met Pete, a local guitarist, and composer he had just hired as a cashier. Pete was also waiting for his big break in music. For the first few months of working with Pete, Ted was impressed with Pete's work ethic and how well he interacted with customers. During lunch, Ted and Pete would often eat together in the store's break room and talk shop about the latest releases, other local bands, upcoming concerts, and, of course, each other's music.*

*But as time went on, Ted began to notice that the lunchtime conversations were increasingly becoming about Pete's music and whenever Ted attempted to talk about his own music or any other subject matter, Pete would quickly divert the conversation back to his own music and the latest songs he had written. To appease Pete, Ted agreed to listen to one of his digital albums and found the music to be horrific and some of the poorest compositions he had ever heard.*

*It wasn't long before Ted grew weary of the one-sided conversations and began avoiding lunch breaks with Pete. Just after Pete's one year anniversary, he left the record store for a better paying job in a warehouse at a tech company. He and Ted exchanged contact information and agreed to stay in touch.*

*However, when Pete reached out to Ted, the encounters were even worse than their lunch breaks had been. Pete spoke only about his music and the latest track he had recorded with his band. Any attempts by Ted to interject about his music or anything else were rudely dismissed by Pete, who would often cut off the conversation once he had exhausted his discussion points.*

*Whenever Ted invited Pete to hear his band play at local clubs, Pete would decline the offer or would simply ignore Ted's texts. To Ted's relief, Pete's attempts to contact him were becoming less frequent.*

*One evening, Ted invited a small group of friends over to celebrate his girlfriend's birthday, and having recently received a call from Pete, he reluctantly invited him to join the celebration. Ted's worst fears were realized when Pete added a playlist without Ted's permission and proceeded to play his music for the guests who were visibly irritated. Ted was livid and asked Pete to leave.*

*The following day, Pete left Ted a message on his voicemail telling Ted how hurt he was that he had been asked to leave the party when all he had wanted was to help celebrate Ted's girlfriend's birthday by generously sharing his music.*

Unfortunately, people like Pete just don't get it, and it's likely they never will. Pete is an emotional Parasite. A Parasite will mooch off of others in a variety of ways until he or she is stopped. Parasites go after whatever their need is that the host friend has: time, money, possessions, or simply a listening ear.

Parasites also come in wide varieties and can be anything from that school buddy, neighbor, or work associate that hangs out with the host friend when there is no one else to hang out with or they may be like Pete, someone who is looking for validation without feeling any responsibility for reciprocity.

I once heard of a woman who often hosted lavish parties, loaned money, and would open her home up to Parasite friends to crash with her when they were in need. When she hit hard times, these same "friends" who had happily accepted this woman's hospitality turned their backs on her when she was in financial need.

While these examples of parasitic friends can leave the host friend feeling hurt and emotionally wounded, not discerning a Parasite friend in time can have deadly results.

Not long ago, I was watching one of my favorite cable channels, Discovery ID, that featured a program about how murder impacts family and friends[1]. The show was about a young man named Bill who had a childhood friend named Larry. The two met in school when they were both 10 and had remained close friends throughout their teen and young adult years. When Bill died in a house fire, Larry was the first to call Bill's sister to share the tragic news.

It was later discovered that Bill had previously given Larry his identification so he could get a job under his name since he allegedly had health problems that made him a liability to prospective employers. After getting Bill's ID, Larry left the state and secured

---

1. Impact of Murder on Discovery ID – "Hearts on Fire" episode - https://www.inv estigationdiscovery.com/tv-shows/impact-of-murder/full-episodes/hearts-on-fire

identification with Bill's details but with Larry's picture. One day, the police stopped the car Larry was driving and after searching, they discovered several pounds of marijuana. The license that Larry shared with the police was the one with his own picture but Bill's details.

Larry assured Bill that he would straighten out the mess he had created in court and asked if he could stay at Bill's place until his court date. Weeks later, the fire happened. Larry was eventually arrested for having a fake ID and while he was in jail, he bragged to a few of his cell mates about burning Bill to death to cover his tracks.

The trusting friend (Bill) had been more than willing to put his neck on the line for his lifelong Parasite friend, Larry, who was not even willing to inconvenience himself but instead, killed his faithful friend to cover his tracks.

This story of a Parasite friend is a sobering reminder about how important it is to carefully vet those we allow into our inner circles and choose as close friends.

### Pros of a 'Parasite' Friend

Unfortunately, there is little advantage or "pro" to having a Parasite friend. These types of people usually start out as fun and outgoing individuals, but in time, their one-directional, demanding ways often overshadow anything positive to be had in the relationship.

### Cons of a 'Parasite' Friend

Most Parasites are narcissistic individuals who are hardwired to be exclusively concerned with their own needs and desires. When they put themselves first, it is not usually out of any malicious intent but truly out of a driven desire to have only their personal needs met. Unfortunately, the friends of a Parasite usually get the short end of the stick.

As was the case with Ted in our first story, the "cons" of the relationship with Pete quickly became obvious. Other than the initial pleasantries that Ted experienced early on in his relationship with Pete, the relationship grew increasingly frustrating for Ted as he got to know Pete better. Rather than a relationship becoming more of a mutual exchange, in the case of a Parasite like Pete, the relationship is bound to become more and more one-sided in favor of the Parasite.

### Signs of a 'Parasite' Friend

A few signs that can suggest that you are dealing with a Parasite include the following:

- Conversations with the person in question increasingly become about them.

- They rarely ask you about your life and if you do interject about your life, they tune you out or simply cut off the conversation.

- You increasingly find yourself giving to this individual but they rarely give back, especially when you express a need.

- The person rarely proactively reaches out to you unless they need something.

**How to Deal with a 'Parasite' Friend**

One dealing with a Parasite must handle this type of friendship with care. In this context, the care I am referring to relates to "self-care," as the Parasite has no regard for anyone except him or herself. Putting up firm boundaries is the first step in dealing with a Parasite. Just as parasitic organisms such as leeches, ticks, or mosquitos do not understand the concept of "enough," a Parasite friend will continue to take from their host friend until the host says "enough" as the Parasite never will.

Only the person in a relationship with a Parasite can determine if he or she will have to put distance between themselves and the friend or even end the friendship if need be. But if well-guarded boundaries are in place, it is possible to maintain a relationship with an individual whose primary mode of operation is to take.

**What if You <u>are</u> a 'Parasite' Friend?**

If after evaluating yourself, you realize that you may have negative qualities that drain the individuals around you, it is important to be sensitive to this. It is natural to be excited about personal opportunities and want to share them with your friend, but when your excitement is routinely one-sided and you are not interested in others, it can be draining. In the case of the individual who only takes, it is hurtful for the one who is always on the short end of the stick and is constantly being taken from.

The best way to stop parasitic behavior is to be mindful of it and when you find yourself engaging in this negative behavior, do just the opposite. For example, if you find yourself constantly dominating discussions with your friend about what is important in your life, make it a point to ask your friend about what is going on in his or her life and restrain yourself from interjecting about what is happening in your life (even if you feel like you'll burst if you don't).

You will definitely surprise your friend and probably yourself as well. You can apply this to other areas where you have concluded you have been domineering in a draining way in the friendship.

# 26

—◆—

# Vampire

*A*lice had just moved out of the apartment she had shared with her boyfriend, Jonas, for one year. She wasn't sure where they were headed as a couple, but Jonas had asked that they take a break from the relationship.

As a result, Alice moved in with her childhood friend, Emma, and Emma's parents. Alice and Emma had been close since they'd met as elementary-aged children, and while Alice was approaching 20, Emma was 17 and entering her senior year of high school.

Emma was initially thrilled to be living under the same roof as her longtime friend, but it was just a matter of weeks before Emma's parents became concerned. Alice was very depressed and her constant dark mood heavily affected the atmosphere in the house.

Believing her good friend's recent breakup with Jonas was the major cause of Alice's mood, Emma encouraged her parents to not worry. Late one evening, Alice confided to Emma that she had been cutting herself and wanted to die.

Emma became very upset and did her best to convince Alice that she indeed had a bright future. The two stayed up until the early morning hours, talking, as both girls cried on and off. By the time the sun came up, Emma was an emotional wreck.

As weeks went by, Alice's mood yo-yoed from ecstatic to very low. Her emotional state had become a rollercoaster for which Emma and her parents found themselves unwittingly forced to ride. Emma also discovered that her own emotions were beginning to mirror Alice's.

One day, Jonas called Alice and told her that he missed her and wanted to take her on a weekend trip.

Believing the breakup with Jonas to be the main source of Alice's depression, Emma implored her friend not to go on the trip and the two argued fiercely, with Alice storming out of the house for the weekend with Jonas.

Emma was deeply hurt by the cruel things Alice had said in the heat of anger and her own emotions took a nosedive that weekend. Emma's parents were not pleased. They had watched *their daughter's normally even-keeled emotional state become as unstable as Alice's during the course of her stay in their home.*

*When Alice returned to Emma's house after the weekend with Jonas, Emma's parents asked her to move out.*

I've encountered quite a few emotional vampires in my life, and just as in our story with Emma and Alice, a vampire friend can be emotionally draining sometimes to the point that you feel the need to do something drastic to address the problem.

I once had a friend that I'll call "Marina" who had been in a long-term friendship with a woman I'll call Gracie. Gracie had been diagnosed with depression and constantly called Marina when she was feeling down, which was often. In time, Marina found herself feeling depressed to the point that she asked her doctor to prescribe medication.

After some probing, her doctor recommended that Marina distance herself from Gracie for a few months and then re-evaluate. Marina followed her doctor's advice and found that all feelings of depression vanished without her taking prescription medication.

In some instances, the only response to a Vampire friend situation is to put some distance between you and the emotionally draining friend.

**Pros of a 'Vampire' Friend**

Most Vampire friends that I've encountered have turned out to be nice people who are generally great to hang out with when their emotions are stable and circumstances in their lives are even. But when life becomes rocky, then look out.

**Cons of a 'Vampire' Friend**

As in the example with Alice and Emma, the worst aspect of the friendship was that Alice's mood swings were negatively affecting the atmosphere in the house and were directly impacting Emma, who began mirroring her friend's dark moods and was feeling the ups and downs along with Alice in a manner that was emotionally unhealthy. The most challenging aspect of having a vampire-like friend is that many need professional help that their friend is not equipped to provide.

**Signs of a 'Vampire' Friend**

A few signs that might suggest that you are dealing with a Vampire include the following:

- You observe that you often feel emotionally low after spending time with them.

- This person is consistently in an emotional low state as a result of a health, personal, or significant relationship in his or her life.

- You often do not hear from him or her when they are in a balanced state or on an emotional high and things are going "well" in their life.

## How to Deal with a 'Vampire' Friend

Befriending or maintaining a friendship with someone who behaves like a Vampire is not out of the question, but establishing clear boundaries is key in dealing successfully with a Vampire friend.

I've known of Vampire friends who have emotionally drained those around them to the point that the friend, like Emma in the example, was beginning to behave as emotionally erratic as the Vampire.

With firm boundaries in place with the Vampire, you have a better chance of preventing the erratic behavior from affecting you.

A few examples of setting healthy boundaries might include:

- *Set specific times as off-limits for the Vampire friend to call* – I once had a Vampire friend who would call me at inappropriate hours to complain about his girlfriend or other woes. After the third time of being awakened after 1:00 am, I told him he was not allowed to call me after 10:00 pm and that if he violated this rule, I would block him.

- *When visiting either in person or via phone with a Vampire friend, limit the length of time you will spend with this person when they are in their emotionally draining periods* – It's best to let him or her know that you only have 10 to 15 minutes to chat. However, if you feel your friend is truly in a dangerously depressed state and might do self-harm, immediately seek professional help on his or her behalf.

- *Think twice about becoming too close with a Vampire friend* – As in the example with Alice and Emma, spending a lot of time with an emotionally draining person can put an emotional strain on you. If your Vampire friend needs a place to stay, try your best to look for options that don't include your home. Unless you are a licensed therapist, you might be better off helping your friend connect with a professional who can help them.

## What if You <u>are</u> a 'Vampire' Friend?

I don't believe anyone intentionally enters a relationship with someone they care about with the goal of taking from that person to such a degree that he or she feels sucked dry.

If you find yourself constantly leaning on your friends emotionally, it sometimes helps to take a step back and put aside your feelings for a minute and put your friend's needs first. This does not mean you should bury your feelings and pretend that everything is all right, but it means that you consciously reach out to your friend to make sure that he or she is okay. Sometimes, just listening to the friend you normally lean on frequently can be enough to lift your gray mood even if just a little.

The bottom line is that you should be able to go to your friends when you are hurting, but you should also strive to keep balance in your friendships and make an effort to not overly burden friends or turn them into your personal therapist. If you continue feeling low or depressed, by all means get the help you deserve by connecting with a professional coach or therapist who may be better equipped to help you.

# 27

## THE TYRANT

*T*rent had just taken a new job as a Group Product Manager for a consumer goods company. He was thrilled about his position because it was a promotion and he would now be managing a team of seven product leads. Up until that point in his career, Trent had been an individual contributor to a technical staff.

He had only been working for the new company for a few weeks when one day he heard shouting through his office wall coming from a deep-voiced male, obviously another manager, who was spewing explicative language at someone in his office. The vehemence of the tirade made Trent shudder. A few minutes later, another manager within the product team dropped by Trent's office and asked him if he'd heard the screaming and explained that it came from the Senior Director of Product Management named "Martin," who was well known for chewing out direct reports on his team. Because Martin led a very profitable product line, upper management turned a blind eye to his foul behavior according to the manager.

A week later, Trent attended a management staff meeting where he was introduced to Martin. To his surprise, Martin seemed like a down-to-earth kind of guy. The two chatted for several minutes before their manager, the Vice President of Products, called the staff meeting to order. When the meeting was over, Martin invited Trent to lunch.

Trent was suspicious of Martin's invitation, but not wanting to get on his bad side, Trent agreed. During lunch, Trent was surprised at how helpful Martin was by giving him the lowdown of how things worked in the company and specifically, how things ran in their department. To Trent's horror, Martin began bad-mouthing several other managers that Trent had met and actually liked, including the manager that had dropped by Trent's office earlier that week. During lunch, the department Vice President dropped by and asked to join them. At one point during their discussion, the Vice President asked Martin about sailing *that Saturday. Martin confirmed that he was still planning to go and he invited Trent to come along.*

*Trent agreed and met Martin and the Vice President early the following Saturday. To Trent's surprise, two people from the executive staff at the company including the CEO showed up to go sailing on Martin's boat. Trent was truly impressed and realized that being associated with Martin definitely had its perks.*

*The following week, Martin came by Trent's office and again invited him to lunch. Since Trent had already accepted a lunch invitation with the manager Martin did not like, Trent politely declined. He and the manager went off-site to lunch at a trendy restaurant and were having a good time until Martin walked in with their Vice President. Trent felt sick with dread and hoped Martin did not see him, but it was too late as Martin made eye contact and did not hide his displeasure.*

*During the next management team meeting, which took place the following Monday, Trent saw Martin sitting at the conference table and said hello. Martin ignored him and continued speaking with another manager. Trent found an empty chair away from Martin and took it. During the meeting, the Vice President brought up a team challenge that nobody wanted to take on and Martin spoke up at once and recommended the challenge be given to Trent. The Vice President seemed pleased with the recommendation. Trent was put on the spot and didn't have a clue as to how to handle the challenge, but being the new guy, he felt he couldn't say no.*

*Later that morning, Martin dropped by Trent's office and apologized for putting him on the spot. To Trent, the apology sounded hollow and more smug than sincere, then Martin blew Trent away when he said he would help Trent with the challenge only if he immediately dropped his association with the manager Martin did not like. Martin said that guy was a loser and he would have no part in helping Trent as long as he associated with him.*

*Trent was in a tough spot. He really liked the manager but knew that getting on Martin's bad side could prove to be career-limiting at the company. He suddenly did not like his new job or Martin.*

You would think that this sort of behavior would stop at high school and would not expect it to take place in the workplace, but unfortunately, it happens. I've witnessed similar variations of Tyrants in the workplace and know what it's like to be under the thumb of someone who behaves more like a dictator.

As was the case with Trent, most people involved in a Tyrant friendship grow to not care for the person who is behaving like an oppressor and the reason they remain in the relationship has little to do with concern for the friend but has more to do with fear of what will happen if they don't comply with the friend's demands. In the case of Trent, addressing Martin's bad behavior could have ostracized him at the company.

**Pros of a 'Tyrant' Friend**

Those who are Tyrant friends usually have something compelling to offer those that they take on as "friends." In the case of Martin and Trent, instant companionship and induction into the elite club were the compelling offers that Martin provided Trent who was new to the company.

Although a Tyrant friend can be made outside of work, they usually can be found in the work environment and usually take place between a co-worker or manager/subordinate situation where the Tyrant in the work situation provides a benefit to his or her employee "friend."

Years ago, I worked for a company where my manager had to interact with a more senior manager in another department who was a Tyrant. This Tyrant was quite unpleasant and did not get along with most of the other managers or his employees. He was quite difficult to deal with and most people were afraid of him. Those who worked for this Tyrant manager were often ridiculed and bullied openly in meetings.

When my manager was experiencing challenges with his new boss, a man that the Tyrant manager did not like, the Tyrant manager and my manager became friends. The Tyrant manager was very helpful and was instrumental in my manager receiving a promotion.

My manager eventually resigned but before he left the company, he confided in me that he was relieved to be leaving so he would no longer have to interact with the Tyrant manager.

**Cons of a 'Tyrant' Friend**

The manipulative and oftentimes, cruel aspect of a Tyrant is the biggest drawback of this friend type. Even if an individual starts out liking or feeling drawn towards a Tyrant, the overly dominating characteristic of this friend type will eventually repel even the most long-suffering individual.

The domineering aspect of this friend type also makes him or her more than just a handful and often, these types of individuals have a difficult time maintaining meaningful, long-term relationships with people who genuinely care for them. The unfortunate aspect of a Tyrant is that they drive many people away and those that remain "friends" with them often have ulterior motives and hope to gain something from the Tyrant or at the expense of the Tyrant.

For those who are friends with a Tyrant, another con of this friend type is that they are not free to be themselves in the relationship. Stepping out of line with a Tyrant friend, such as when Trent declined lunch with Martin, so he could keep his lunch date with the manager Martin did not like, can result in negative consequences as Trent experienced.

**Signs of a 'Tyrant' Friend**

It isn't difficult to determine whether or not you are dealing with a Tyrant friend. If you consistently feel unduly pressured by your friend in a manner that makes you uncomfortable, you might be dealing with a Tyrant.

Here are a few other signs that suggest you might be dealing with a Tyrant:

- He or she routinely dominates those around them.

- You witness them blatantly disrespecting other people who fear them.

- They constantly attempt to control the things you do, the things you say, and even the way you think.

- If you attempt to defy a suggestion or an order from this friend, they exact revenge on you.

- You fantasize about the day when you are no longer friends with this person.

If the person in question displays <u>any</u> of the traits described in the bullets above, you may likely be dealing with a Tyrant.

**How to Deal with a 'Tyrant' Friend**

Sometimes, your situation may leave you with no other choice but to remain in a relationship with a Tyrant for a season. As was the case between Trent and Martin, the workplace environment was that situation where Trent felt forced into a relationship with Martin. Trent's worst fear was that he would fall out of favor with all the key players at the company including his boss, the Vice President, and end up being ostracized with his career growth stunted.

For many people involved with a Tyrant friend either at school, work, or in a personal situation, the circumstances drawing them together with the Tyrant is the glue holding together the relationship. It is often just a matter of waiting out that situation.

Regarding Trent's case, if either he or Martin left the company, Trent's problem with the Tyrant, Martin, would likely be over.

In the example I gave earlier with my former manager having to interact with another manager who was a Tyrant, my manager's challenges with this Tyrant manager were over once he left the company.

However, if you do not have the luxury of waiting out a situation and it looks like your relationship with the Tyrant does not have an end date; you may want to consider a more proactive approach than simply toughing out the situation until it comes to a natural end. Bear in mind that you may have to be direct with your Tyrant.

If you feel that you can or need to take more direct control over your situation with a Tyrant, make sure you are physically and emotionally safe, and in the instance of a work situation with a Tyrant friend, make sure you are professionally safe before confronting the Tyrant.

Before confronting the Tyrant, make sure you have already set clear boundaries of what is and is not acceptable for how the Tyrant treats you. If you have not yet set clear boundaries, you need to decide what those boundaries are before having that tough talk with the Tyrant.

Here are a few other tips to consider before taking the confrontational approach with the Tyrant:

- Be direct with the Tyrant about your boundaries and make it clear that crossing those boundaries are not acceptable.

- Have a backup plan for what you will say or do if the Tyrant becomes hostile.

- Decide in advance what you will do if the Tyrant continues to behave inappropriately with you and stick to that plan of action.

### What if You <u>are</u> a 'Tyrant' Friend?

If after reading the Signs of a Tyrant friend section, you see yourself reflected in a few of the descriptions and you are comfortable with that, great. You can ignore the advice below and move to the next friend type.

If, however, you are not comfortable with friends fearing you, dreading being in your presence, and praying for the day they no longer have to deal with you, then, seriously consider making an effort to modify your behavior in a manner that is respectful to those who you call friends.

A lighthearted discussion with a friend might be a good starting point to ask them if you have crossed a line. If appropriate in your situation, apologize and make an effort to stop crossing those lines.

Most people desire to have friends and allies in their lives who genuinely like them and want to be in their presence, even in the workplace. Most do not want to feel imprisoned and looking for an escape hatch from the friendship.

Decide today that you will honor the boundaries that your friends set without seeking to punish them for setting boundaries. If you aren't certain what the boundaries are, you can ask in a subtle way.

You don't have to go through life dominating your friends. If you really desire to have caring people in your life who are there because they want to be, then be prepared to show them respect.

# 28

## THE ROYAL FRIEND

*A*my moved across the country to start her first real job after graduating college. She took an entry-level coordinator position in the marketing department of a large, well-known firm where she met Kate, a marketing specialist who worked in her department.

Kate was just a few years older than Amy and was very helpful. Kate helped her quickly adjust to the new job as well as the new city that Amy had just moved to. It was very easy to talk to Kate, who was well-liked and seemed to get along with almost everyone at the company.

Amy noticed that just about everyone – guys and girls – who met Kate, gushed over her and went out of their way to be generous and friendly. In Amy's opinion, Kate was the proverbial "belle of the ball."

One day, an employee at the company was transferred to the marketing department to take another specialist role on the team. True to form, Kate was very friendly and welcoming to the new transfer, Callie. Amy also befriended Callie and discovered that she really enjoyed spending time working with her and even began hanging out with Callie outside of the office. Whereas Amy, who had regularly eaten lunch with Kate and sometimes others that Kate invited to come along, now began eating lunch with just Callie.

But as Amy and Callie's friendship developed, Amy noticed that Kate began scrutinizing her work more closely than what seemed reasonable to Amy and began increasing her workload.

One day, Callie took Amy aside and shared with her that Kate had said some rather unflattering things about Amy to her and had indicated that Kate had mentioned that she planned to bring these unflattering things to upper management. Sure enough, a senior manager called Amy into his office to address the issues Kate had brought to him and Amy was written up for a poor job performance.

*Amy was disgusted with Kate as the complaints expressed were not that serious and certainly did not warrant escalation. In an attempt to diffuse the problem, Amy invited Kate to lunch to clear the air.*

*During the lunch, Kate seemed elated to be spending time alone with Amy and they got along so well that Amy had a difficult time comprehending how this seemingly sweet woman would have put her job in jeopardy over such trivial matters. When Amy brought up the issue that had gotten her into trouble with management, Kate promised to help Kate improve her work and assured Amy that she would do everything in her power to help her succeed in her role at the company.*

*Amy was relieved that she and Kate seemed to be back on track, but she no longer trusted Kate. Not long after that, Amy heard through another employee that the company's IT manager had gotten into trouble for allegedly sexually harassing Kate, and he, too, had been written up and his job was now in jeopardy. As Amy reflected on the situation between Kate and the IT manager, she recalled how he had frequently stopped by Kate's cube to flirt with her and Kate did not seem to have minded.*

*But recently, a new pretty girl in accounting had caught the IT manager's eye and he had begun spending time with her. Rumor had it that the IT manager and the new girl in accounting had become exclusive and the IT manager no longer dropped by to flirt with Kate. Amy wondered if there was any connection between the IT manager shifting his attention to the new girl and Kate's sudden accusation of sexual harassment.*

*From then on, Amy decided to go out of her way to be nice and flattering to Kate, to make it a point to invite her to lunch at least once a week, and to always accept Kate's invitations for lunch. When it came time for Amy's next performance review, she received glowing marks from Kate.*

I have run into a few "Kates" in my lifetime. I call this type the "Royal" friend, as this person treats those within his or her circle as their subjects, who have the sole purpose of pleasing them and doing their bidding.

When it comes to showing genuine friendship to their subjects, it depends on how much the Royal friend desires to give. Most people involved in a Royal friendship are often okay with the relationship at the beginning, but as time goes on and they do something displeasing to the Royal friend, they can be in for a rude awakening.

### Pros of a 'Royal' Friend

Those who fit into this friend category are typically outgoing, charismatic, and likable individuals. Royal friends also have the gift of quickly drawing in new people and making them feel at ease, special, and included in the group. In our story of Kate and Amy, Kate not only made Amy a part of her circle of friends, proactively helping her acclimate to the marketing team, but she also spent time with her outside of work and showed her around the city.

Meeting this type of friend can initially be exhilarating. Like many of the other friend types discussed in *Friend Encyclopedia*, Royal friends are very personable individuals who often possess the gift of conveying trustworthiness. This can be problematic for the individual who has shared confidential information with the Royal friend and has now fallen out of favor with them.

### Cons of a 'Royal' Friend

The biggest drawback of a Royal friend occurs when he or she feels they are losing control of the affections of their friend, which can be perceived as disloyal. When I say disloyal in the context of a Royal friend, I am not necessarily referring to an actual betrayal, but to a perceived behavior that to a Royal friend may feel like a betrayal.

Amy branching out and befriending others on the team was the catalyst for Kate to feel betrayed. To someone who is not a Royal friend, Amy extending friendship to another would not be a big deal, but in fact, it might be perceived as a good thing. In the mind of a Royal friend, this branching out could be perceived as treasonous.

When it appeared that Amy preferred spending lunch and after work time with Callie, Kate was clearly bothered and responded by bringing a negative report of Amy's work performance to management.

Had Amy continued regularly spending lunch and after work time with Kate and had paid little attention to Callie, Kate likely would not have brought up her work performance to management. And had there actually been a problem with Amy's work performance, Kate would have likely dealt one-on-one with Amy, addressing and giving her pointers to improve.

The worst aspect of a Royal friend is that they have unrealistic expectations of their friends and what they demand from them is not usually reciprocated. In other words, they expect their friends to do extraordinary things to please them but feel no obligation to go out of their way for them in any meaningful way.

### Signs of a 'Royal' Friend

Because Royal friends are initially personable and easy to deal with, the beginning interactions with this friend type usually begin blissfully and the unassuming friend might not have a clue of what they are about to encounter until the friendship matures.

However, once a Royal friend begins to show signs, it isn't hard to decipher. Here are a few signs that you might be dealing with a Royal friend.

- You notice that other friends of this individual seem to be enamored with them, sometimes to the point of worshiping them.

- He or she regularly receives generosity from you and others, but they rarely reciprocate with equal generosity.

- Will manipulate a situation to make sure he or she remains in the spotlight.

- Often is the center of attention and appears troubled if someone else receives attention.

- If you have previously been generous with your attention towards this person and redirect your attention to another, then negative consequences follow.

**How to Deal with a 'Royal' Friend**

How you deal with a Royal friend depends on your comfort level with respect to giving the undivided attention that is necessary to keep this friend type happy. Some people are okay with what could be described as a lopsided relationship where one person invests a lot of time, support, and care into a friend and receives little in return. Others may not be okay with it, but they find themselves in a Royal friend relationship that cannot be immediately addressed.

If you find yourself in a Royal friend relationship, it's important for you to be aware that you likely will not receive the same level of attention that you consistently provide to your friend. You should not be shocked if the time comes that you have a great need in your life and your Royal friend does not come through for you or show the consideration that you would have shown them if they were in your predicament.

If you feel the need to address a Royal friend about their behavior, just know that this person may retaliate in the future. If you decide that confronting this person is necessary, the best time to address a problem with your Royal friend is while he or she is displaying bad behavior.

Our example between Kate and Amy might not be the best example to use because Amy's job was on the line and there was a limit to how honest she could have been with Kate. Additionally, Amy no longer trusted Kate after Kate had reported her to the management for no good reason.

Because of Amy's situation at work, she had to be very careful in how she approached Kate. Had this been a social situation instead of a work situation, Amy might have put space between herself and Kate and let the friendship die a natural death if she no longer trusted her and did not want to continue being friends.

However, if Amy was indeed interested in being friends with Kate, she could share with Kate how she felt about her going behind her back and putting her in a bad light with management. Kate's response in this instance should be the deciding factor of whether or not Amy continues being friends with her. If, for instance, Kate became argumentative and refused to take responsibility for reporting Amy, then Amy would know that the relationship would not likely improve and it would be a matter of time before Kate did something worse.

But if Kate were to take responsibility for her actions and apologize to Amy, there is a chance that they could work on their friendship together and be successful.

As with most friend types, boundaries are key when dealing with a Royal friend. In advance of confronting your Royal friend, you will have to determine what you will or will not be willing to put up with from this person. If you notice there isn't any change after you have spoken with your friend about their bad behavior, then you will likely have to put distance between yourselves or end the friendship, tacitly or directly.

### What if You are a "Royal' Friend?

It might be hard to admit that you could be a Royal friend, but if after reading the Signs of a Royal friend section, you've concluded that you might be this friend type, then take heart; it's not the end of the world.

Be aware that you tend to be self-absorbed and work on being more reciprocal with your friends. If you truly care about your circle of friends, then you will have to proactively nurture those relationships. If you have a friend that always remembers your birthday and gives you a gift, make it a point to set a reminder on your calendar and wish him/her a Happy Birthday and send a gift.

If your devoted friend normally splurges on you for your birthday but you are not in a financial position to return the favor, do what you can according to your means. It is the thought that counts.

If your friend makes it a point to ask you about what's happening in your life, surprise her by asking her what's happening in their life, too. Set a goal to operate on a "two-way street," where both you and your friend do positive things for one another. Steer clear of operating in a "one-way street" manner where your friend does for you and you happily receive and do little in return.

# 29

## PORTA POTTY

*V*ance was a senior auditor with a government agency who had just been given a new manager, Glenn, who was greatly feared for his reputation as having an acid tongue and a vindictive streak.

Initially, Vance dreaded the thought of reporting to Glenn and wondered if he should seriously look into being transferred. But within a short period, it was apparent that Glenn genuinely liked Vance and was going out of his way to mentor him.

At first, the frequent lunches and offers to spend time with the boss outside of work were met with gladness. But months into the intense one-sided bonding, Vance became weary of Glenn whose constant invitations felt intrusive. It wasn't long before Vance loathed Glenn and found him to be a disgusting human being that he dreaded spending time with.

After a serious discussion with his wife, Vance decided to leave his position with the agency to focus on finding a new job. Before he was able to give notice, Glenn told Vance that he was promoting him to senior supervisor and expanding his team. While Vance was excited about the unexpected promotion, he was well aware that it came with strings. He reluctantly accepted his new responsibilities and prepared himself for Glenn to serve as a puppeteer. But Vance was not prepared for the barrage of daily lunch invitations or the offers for Vance and his family to spend time on the weekends with Glenn and his partner at their cabin.

Within a year, Vance had once again decided to leave his job. On the day he had planned to submit his resignation, Glenn dropped a bomb that he had given notice and was leaving the agency by the end of the month.

Vance was thrilled. He could now remain in his position and the everyday lunches and excruciating weekends with Glenn were behind him.

But nobody was as surprised as Vance when the invitations from Glenn for lunch and family get-togethers continued after he had left the agency almost with the same regularity as they had when he was still his manager.

*While Vance tried to graciously decline the offers, the rejections went right over Glenn's head. He just didn't seem to get that Vance was not interested. Vance tried ignoring emails and phone calls but that didn't work because Glenn simply called him at his work desk from a private number.*

*With extra time on his hands, Glenn's pursuit of Vance was unrelenting. Weeks following Glenn's departure from the agency, Vance decided that a clean break and a drastic new direction was needed. He resigned from his position, changed his home and mobile numbers, and put his house up for sale.*

It's unfortunate when you try your best to let someone know in the kindest and most subtle way possible that you are not interested, but they just don't get it. In many cases, such as was with Vance and Glenn, drastic measures are an order.

Years ago, I participated in a walk-a-thon for the Muscular Dystrophy Association. I had been walking for hours in the hot sun and was growing thirstier by the minute. McDonald's had sponsored a refreshment station and was providing free orange sodas. I was so thirsty I grabbed three cups and quickly drank them. About an hour later, I was beginning to feel the after-effect of guzzling down three sodas, back-to-back and there was no bathroom in sight.

Every minute that passed was torture as I searched the streets for a restaurant or store that would allow walkers to use their bathroom facilities. I was about to abandon the idea of finding a bathroom and look for a bush when I spotted a Porta-Potty with a small line of walkers waiting to use it. That Porta-Potty was like a desert oasis and I was grateful to have found it. At that moment in time, the Porta-Potty was my best friend.

While the Porta-Potty was a godsend during my walk-a-thon, the idea of using one during my everyday life is not something I would ever consider unless I was in desperate need.

I was recently heading to a restaurant and found myself sitting in evening traffic longer than expected. I needed to use the bathroom before sitting down for dinner. On my way into the restaurant, I noticed a Porta-Potty in the parking garage. It never occurred to me to use it when I knew there was a nice clean bathroom waiting for me inside the restaurant.

Some friendships with certain individuals can feel just like that Porta-Potty. In a dire situation, the particular friend might seem like a flash snow storm during a heat wave, but if the situation is not dire, the last thing you want is to spend time with that person.

**Pros of a 'Porta-Potty' Friend**

There really is only one "pro" to having a Porta-Potty friend and that is they are meeting a present need during a period in your life. These are usually individuals who are far more interested in you than you are in them. In most cases, a Porta-Potty friend is faithful to you during a tough situation and can be counted on to support you.

**Cons of a 'Porta-Potty' Friend**

This type of friendship has an expiration date that terminates when the dire situation bringing you together comes to an end. Unlike a Foxhole friend, there usually isn't an emotional connection or desire to continue a relationship with the Porta-Potty friend any longer than necessary. When the dire situation bringing you together with the Porta-Potty is over, you look for the exit while the Porta-Potty friend, like Glenn, attempts to continue in the friendship.

It might sound cruel to place someone into this unpleasant category, but there usually is an underlying reason that this individual makes you feel uncomfortable and you should not feel obligated to override your feelings or to force yourself into a relationship with this person that you don't like.

In the example with Vance and Glenn, Vance grew increasingly repulsed by his manager the more time he spent time with him. This was not a situation that just needed more time to work itself out; Vance detested Glenn and there was nothing that could change that.

As far as Vance was concerned, the friendship was over the moment Glenn resigned from the agency. Unfortunately, many Porta-Potty friends are often so enamored with their friend that they are not ready to disengage once the dire situation is over.

As was the case for Vance and Glenn, Glenn was ready to kick the friendship into high gear after leaving the agency while Vance was long over it.

**Signs of a 'Porta-Potty' Friend**

Generally speaking, a Porta-Potty friend is someone who makes you feel uncomfortable, uneasy, and in some instances, disgusted and sickened by their presence. Sometimes, these feelings are legitimate, meaning this person has done something negative to you or to someone you know, but oftentimes these feelings of repulsion are unfounded and cannot tie back to anything in particular.

Here are a few signs of a Porta-Potty friend:

- You really don't like this person

- The thought of spending time with this person causes you to feel uneasy, angry, or makes your skin crawl

- Outside of the situation that you are pulled into with this person, you do not want to spend time with them

- Bottom line: You can't wait to get away from this person.

I am a firm believer in respecting your feelings. If you really are uncomfortable being around someone that you believe is a Porta-Potty friend, then you should do what you can to minimize the time spent with that person.

### How to Deal with a 'Porta-Potty' Friend

Unlike some friend types that may not necessarily be positive but you can still engage with that friend, I do not recommend that you try cultivating a relationship with a Porta-Potty friend. The visceral reaction you have to this type of person is there for a reason and should not be ignored.

If you assess that this individual is basically harmless, they just happen to get on your nerves. It might be a good idea to treat them with casual friendliness when they reach out to you, but you should not be proactive with this person or give any signs of encouragement.

However, if you find this person to be unpleasant or offensive, you should avoid spending time with them at all cost as any time that you devote to them might be construed as interest in friendship

### What if You are a 'Porta-Potty' Friend?

It's difficult to come to terms with the fact that someone might not want to be friends with you the way you may want to be friends with them, but that is the painful reality for the person who _is_ deemed a Porta-Potty Friend.

It's most important to observe the signs your friend is giving you. If they constantly reject you, perhaps stop pursuing them.

Here are a few signs that you might be viewed as a Porta-Potty friend:

- You are always the initiator in inviting your friend to do things, and your invitations are politely refused or ignored.

- Your friend in question never invites you to participate in group or one-on-one activities.

- Your friend never initiates phone calls, emails, or texts and rarely responds when you call or text.

- If you did not reach out to your friend, you might not ever hear from them.

If you answer yes to any of the above bullets, you may want reassess your friendship with this person. If you determine you are indeed the Porta-Potty in this relationship, by all means, don't confront or accuse this person, and above all, don't beat yourself up! Friends are not "*one size fits all*." Even though this friend may not appreciate you, there is another friend out there who would be thrilled to have you. Walk away from any relationship where you are not valued with your dignity intact and determine that you will offer your generous friendship to someone else who will appreciate it and be truly delighted to have you as a friend.

# 30

## TOXIC WASTE

*A* aliyah had just joined a new gym. After having thrown herself into her career for so long, she noticed she had put on a few extra pounds and decided to jump in with both feet with a new workout schedule, which meant she would be at the gym five days a week.

On her first day of the Crossfit class she had signed up for, Aaliyah met Rosemary, a young woman who was also in her mid-20s like Aaliyah. Rosemary took Aaliyah under her wing and was very friendly. The two became workout partners in class.

It wasn't a surprise to Aaliyah when Rosemary suggested they should hang out sometime outside of the gym. Aaliyah was open to the suggestion and they planned for lunch that Saturday afternoon. During the lunch, when Aaliyah ordered extra crispy French fries to go with her hamburger, Rosemary criticized Aaliyah's food choices. When Aaliyah protested that she had worked out pretty hard that week at the gym and wanted a little splurge, Rosemary didn't back off one bit. Throughout the meal, she continued relentlessly putting down Aaliyah and told her that if she ever wanted to be able to touch her toes again she'd better give up her bad eating habits. The comments made Aaliyah feel like garbage.

During the rest of the meal, Rosemary made fun of other restaurant patrons that were out of shape or overweight, telling Aaliyah if she didn't watch it, she'd wind up like one of them.

The following week at the gym, Rosemary brought up Aaliyah's fattening Saturday meal a few times during their tough workouts to the point where Aaliyah became fed up by the comments, and the next time Rosemary made a rude comment about her weight, Aaliyah called her on it.

Rosemary shrugged Aaliyah's comment off and told Aaliyah that she was just messing with her and to not take her seriously. She eased up on teasing Aaliyah for the rest of that workout, but the next day, when Rosemary was assisting Aaliyah during sit-ups, she made *a loud comment to Aaliyah about how foul her breath was and maybe if she didn't eat so poorly, her breath wouldn't smell like someone had just taken a dump in her mouth.*

*That Friday when Rosemary asked Aaliyah if she wanted to catch the new release of a movie that was premiering that day, Aaliyah lied and said that she already had plans.*

It can be so disappointing to meet a new friend with whom you feel you have a lot in common only to discover that the person has a mean streak that's often directed towards you and you can't get away from them fast enough. Such was the case in our story between Aaliyah and Rosemary.

While my personal encounters with Toxic Waste friends have been minimal, I have heard stories from others that have been mind boggling. A girl I know told me a story about when she was in high school and how she had a friend that she really liked at first, but in time, the friend constantly put her down and called her names. The bad behavior did not just stop at verbal assaults, as the friend would at times be so insulting that their exchanges would turn into fierce arguments that would often end with the insulting friend hitting her!

Most Toxic Waste individuals that I've observed aren't as drastic as resorting to physical violence and usually are only verbally offensive, but like Rosemary, these individuals usually start on the surface as decent friends but their verbal insults or other intrusive ways can take a friendship that starts out promising and turn it into something so foul that the one on the receiving end of the insults cannot get away from the Toxic Friend fast enough.

### Pros of a 'Toxic Waste' Friend

Toxic Waste friends often have positive character traits that make them initially attractive. They are often charismatic and personable individuals that are fun to be around and start out by making a person feel safe and comfortable in their presence. Most people with even a small degree of self-esteem would not accept a friend who right out of the gate put them down or made fun of them. Toxic Waste friends usually present a positive side that starts out as fun. In our story, Rosemary was so friendly and helpful towards Aaliyah in class to the degree that when she invited Aaliyah to lunch, Aaliyah did not hesitate to say yes. It wasn't until Aaliyah was comfortable in the new budding friendship that Rosemary began showing her true colors.

### Cons of a 'Toxic Waste' Friend

In time, Toxic Waste friends will eventually reveal their true negative character and will begin hurling insults directed at friends once the friend's guard is down. The worst part of a Toxic Waste friend is that it rarely stops at the occasional put-down, which could probably be overlooked provided it was a rare occurrence. With a Toxic Waste friend, the insults or rude comments are consistent. As it was between Aaliyah and Rosemary, when Aaliyah told Rosemary that her insults were offensive, Rosemary backed off only long enough to lunge into another insult that was even crueler than her original ribbing about Aaliyah ordering French fries.

A Toxic Waste friend can be relentless to the point that the friend on the receiving end of their insults will distance themselves from the friendship or simply end it.

**Signs of a 'Toxic Waste' Friend**

The person involved in a Toxic Waste friendship often feels controlled by the cruel and insulting behavior they receive from this friend type. The signature sign of being in the presence of a Toxic Waste friend is that this person whom you originally enjoyed hanging out with now makes you want to avoid them because of the abusive way they treat you.

Here are a few other signs of a Toxic Waste friend:

- The friend that you really like has started putting you down and when you ask them to stop, they don't.

- Your friend is hyper-critical of you in a manner that makes you feel uncomfortable and insecure.

- You observe your friend making vicious comments about others behind their back on an ongoing basis.

- Whenever you are around your friend, you feel bad about yourself because of the things he or she says to you.

- You dread getting together with this person because of the mean things he or she says to you.

If your friend's behavior is something that makes you feel bad about yourself and you dread spending time with them, then pay attention to those feelings and consider taking steps to address this problem.

**How to Best Deal with a 'Toxic Waste' Friend**

The best course of action when dealing with a Toxic Waste friend is to be as direct as you can with this person and let them know that their behavior towards you is unacceptable and will not be tolerated. In our story, Aaliyah's approach to Rosemary demonstrated the kinder side of direct and was even gentle in comparison to Rosemary's abrasive insults.

By explaining to Rosemary that her attacking her food choices with insults hurt her feelings was a delicate way of asking Rosemary to back off. Although Aaliyah could have been much more direct and told Rosemary to mind her own business or she could have resorted to giving back insults, Aaliyah instead took the high road. In my opinion, Aaliyah's approach to Rosemary was a softball response.

However, Rosemary just didn't get it or just chose to ignore. Aaliyah's dismissing Rosemary's invitation to see a movie by lying that she already had plans is an okay response. Since Aaliyah was in the early stages of building a friendship with Rosemary, she did not owe her a more substantial explanation. Had she and Rosemary already built a friendship and had weathered a few things together, a more truthful talk about Rosemary's behavior would have been appropriate. Since the friendship was still in its beginning stages, Aaliyah gently backing off was a safe approach.

Many people do not like confrontations and would prefer to respond the way Aaliyah did by explaining to the offending friend how their behavior makes them feel, and like Aaliyah, they will not feel comfortable with taking a harsher approach and giving back as severely as they are getting.

If that describes you, then like Aaliyah, gently backing away from a Toxic Waste friend is the way to go if your delicate approach of asking them nicely to stop insulting you does not deter them.

Using the example of Aaliyah and Rosemary, here are a few levels of responses you can consider if you are in a similar situation with a Toxic Waste Friend who constantly insults you:

- Gentle – Share with your Toxic Waste friend that when they say mean things to you, it hurts your feelings.

- More Direct – Tell your Toxic Waste friend that you do not like it when they say insulting things to you and you would like them to stop.

- Fully Direct – Tell your Toxic Waste friend that they will stop with the insults effective immediately or there will be consequences.

- Over the top – Tell your Toxic Waste friend that they are offensive, you are not putting up with their disgusting behavior any longer and you are done with them, effective now (and mean it).

## What if You <u>are</u> a 'Toxic Waste' Friend?

If after reading the Aaliyah/Rosemary story and the "signs of" section and you see some similarities between you and Rosemary, then you should consider if you might be showing some Toxic Waste traits. It may not be your intention to make your friends feel insulted and put down but that may be what you are unknowingly doing.

If you think back to recent or past interactions with friends and recall maybe a strange look a friend gave you or something someone said that might indicate that you have been overbearing to some degree, then consider what you can do to stop this behavior.

Knowing that you may have the tendency to put down your friends is the first step in getting control over this behavior, so you don't cause your friends to become wary of you and eventually avoid you or worse, cut you out of their life.

If you believe you might have a tendency to be a Toxic Waste friend, then make sure you carefully watch your behavior. When interacting with your friend, pause before responding to something they say to make sure you are not about to say something insulting or hurtful. Sometimes, just taking a moment or two to think about what you say can keep you from saying something that you'll later regret.

Even if you think what you are saying to your friend is not a big deal, bear in mind that it isn't so much what you think but how your friend feels about what you say.

At the end of the day, if you strive to be a good friend and have good friendships, you will make sure that you make your friends feel comfortable and safe around you, which will lead them to wanting to spend time with you because they genuinely like being around you.

# 31

## DANGEROUS LIAISON

*R*yan had just moved into a new apartment building. Having recently broken up with his live-in girlfriend, he was making a new start and on his own for the first time in years. He had never had many guy friends, to begin with, since he was almost always in a romantic relationship. Because most of his few guy friends were part of a couple and were also friends of his ex, Ryan found himself with very few friends at this point in his life.

Not long after Ryan had moved into the new apartment, a guy moved into the unit directly across from Ryan's. The guy, Carson, was about as opposite from Ryan's straight-laced and buttoned-down appearance as night and day. Carson had several piercings, full-sleeve tattoos, wore leathers, and rode a loud Harley. He seemed dangerous and this intrigued Ryan.

Whenever Ryan heard Carson's Harley pulling into the carport, he'd turn off the lights in his apartment, sneak over to his living room window and watch Carson enter his apartment. Finally, after watching his neighbor for several weeks, Ryan worked up the nerve to introduce himself. Having once seen Carson carrying a bottle of Samuel Adams beer, Ryan purchased a six-pack of it and knocked on Carson's door.

Carson accepted the welcome gift and invited Ryan inside. The two drank and got to know each other. Carson came across as a down-to-earth guy who said he worked in construction and was also a member of a motorcycle gang. Ryan told him that he had recently gotten out of a six-year relationship and was feeling a little out of his element. To Ryan's surprise, Carson invited him to hang out that Friday at a local bar with him and his motorcycle buddies.

Ryan was thrilled at the idea of hanging out with bikers. That Friday evening, he met Carson at the seedy bar and found that his motorcycle buddies were so much more exciting than Ryan's other friends, most of whom he had shared with his ex.

*As the night wore on, Ryan, who was not used to heavy drinking, was drunker than he had been since the height of his partying days in college. He was way past tipsy and had lost all inhibitions as he shamelessly flirted with every woman within close range. The attractive, scantily dressed waitress that regularly came by to refill their drinks was a prime target of Ryan's leering eyes and busy hands. Carson and his buddies were amused and a little surprised by how this slightly nerdy guy had become such a wild man. When a beautiful woman walked past the table where they sat, Ryan grabbed the woman's ass.*

*Within seconds, a tough biker guy stormed over to the table and began roughing up Ryan. Carson and his buddies came to Ryan's rescue and it wasn't long before a bar brawl ensued. Ryan managed to crawl away from the scuffle and hid in a corner not knowing what else to do. He had never been in a fist fight before and was completely out of his element.*

*Minutes later, police sirens pierced through the air. Several bikers scattered from the bar. Ryan made his way back over to the table where he had been sitting with Carson and his buddies where he found Carson sprawled on the ground, bleeding profusely from his abdomen.*

You can't judge a book by its cover. Oftentimes, a person may appear to be one way on the outside and may actually be completely different on the inside once you get to know him or her. Ryan assumed that Carson was a dangerous guy based on his rough exterior of piercings and tattoos when inside Carson was really a nice, loyal, and down-to-earth guy who took pity on Ryan for having recently broken up with his ex.

Never would Carson have imagined that Ryan would be the one responsible for him being left with a life-threatening wound.

The Dangerous Liaison friend is someone that you least expect to put you in danger. If you are not watching for the subtle signs in this person's behavior, you can find yourself in a compromising situation that could put you in danger

### Pros of a 'Dangerous Liaison' Friend

The pro for this type of friend is that they bring quality to one's life that is vastly different from traits they personally possess. These traits can be varying degrees of fun and excitement and are almost always traits that are opposite to yours.

For Ryan, the edginess of Carson's appearance was alluring while for Carson who spent a lot of time with edgy guys, the idea of hanging out with straight-laced Ryan was the draw.

Let's face it, most of us, if we met someone and immediately felt that they would put us in danger, we would never engage with that person, but with a Dangerous Liaison friend, the allure of these unusual opposing qualities appears fun and exciting and offer balance into your life that can be very attractive.

### Cons of a 'Dangerous Liaison' Friend

The subtlety of the Dangerous Liaison friend can be the most difficult aspect of discerning this friend type. In our story, Ryan appeared like a harmless nerdy guy, who initially served as a refreshing difference between the edgy Carson and his biker buddies. The danger that Ryan put Carson and his friends in was not readily obvious until Ryan became sloppy drunk and threw off his inhibitions. Once the uninhibited Ryan came out to play, the danger presented itself to Carson and his friends. Had Carson and his biker buddies been paying closer attention, they could have perhaps diffused an otherwise dangerous situation before it became an out-of-hand bar brawl.

### Signs of a 'Dangerous Liaison' Friend

As stated previously, the signs for the Dangerous Liaison can be very subtle in many cases. Had Ryan not been drinking heavily, it is possible that his dangerous tendencies may not have been presented.

On the flip side, the situation could also have gone in a different direction. Let's say that instead of Carson being an all-around nice guy, he had a temper problem and became easily angry. Perhaps he would have been the one to pick a fight with one of the other bikers at the bar, putting Ryan in danger.

But in this story, Ryan was the Dangerous Liaison who displayed signs to Carson and his buddies that should have been noted when his demeanor dramatically changed after he'd had a few drinks and flirted with the lines of decency with every woman that came near the table.

Given that they were in a biker bar and noting how rowdy Ryan was rapidly becoming, the other guys should have warned him to settle down or should have perhaps taken him out of the bar before he crossed the line with the woman whose behind he grabbed unaware that she was there with another biker.

In a practical sense, there are signs of a Dangerous Liaison that you should be on the lookout for when engaging with a new person. Most importantly, you should observe how they interact with you and with others. Here are a few signs that should raise a red flag that you may be dealing with a Dangerous Liaison:

- The person shows flashes of dark behavior that are contrary to what you normally see.

- This person shows subtle or not-so-subtle signs of argumentativeness with others.

- You witness this person actually engaging in questionable or illegal behavior.

- Shows signs that he or she likes to start trouble.

- You have a gut feeling that something is not right.

This friend type does not just apply to someone like Ryan who may not be able to handle the drink but can apply to a variety of situations with a new person who could potentially place you in an undesirable position.

Years ago, I befriended a woman who initially was very likable and seemed like a lot of fun. I had no idea she was naturally combative and regularly complained and argued with virtually everyone. I went to dinner with her and soon discovered this unpleasant trait of hers. I had been to this particular restaurant many times and always enjoyed the experience, but my new friend was unnecessarily belligerent to our waiter and had issues with everything about the restaurant.

We ended up leaving in a not-so-nice way. I was so embarrassed by my friend's behavior that I never ate at that restaurant again. While this example is not what I would consider mortal danger in any way, I consider it a different type of danger in terms of my reputation.

**How to Deal with a 'Dangerous Liaison' Friend**

When engaging with a new person that could potentially become a friend, there can be a tendency to be a little extra lenient and excuse poor behavior. This is because you don't want to appear judgmental and, after all, you want this person to like you, but this can be a mistake especially as it relates to the Dangerous Liaison friend. It often may not be clear at first that you are dealing with someone who could put you in danger, so it's best to keep your eyes open so you can make the discovery before it's too late.

Dealing directly with this person should happen the moment you witness a dramatic change. In our story of Ryan and Carson, after Ryan had flirted a few times with the women near their table, Carson should have gently reminded him that some of these women might be with someone at the bar and that he should settle down before he gets himself into trouble.

If that didn't calm Ryan down, then a more direct approach should have been taken such as moving tables away from Ryan. That would probably have been enough to ease his rowdiness. If Ryan's bad behavior continued to escalate, the final straw could have been for Carson to call a cab for Ryan, send him home to sober up, and not hang out with him again.

The point in this example and other Dangerous Liaison situations is to be observant of the new friend's behavior and make note of any major changes that could affect the situation that you are in with this person. Here are a few general tips for dealing directly with a Dangerous Liaison friend:

- Upon witnessing behavior from this person that makes you feel uneasy, gently ask this person to stop the behavior.

- Be prepared to more directly address this person to change their behavior if it appears their behavior could place you in danger.

- Create a plan B in advance just in case this person's behavior does not change or grows worse.

In the event that a new person, such as a Ryan-type, places you in a dangerous situation, you should not feel any obligation to continue building a friendship with that individual. If I had been in Carson's shoes (that is if Carson recovered from his life-threatening wound), I would have nothing more to do with Ryan.

**What if You <u>are</u> a 'Dangerous Liaison' Friend?**

Most people who meet a potential friend that they like a lot strive to impress that person. Unfortunately, there are times when engaging with someone new, especially someone who may be radically different from you, can backfire, especially if you are trying too hard.

If after reading the Ryan/Carson story and reviewing the signs of a Dangerous Liaison, you can see familiarity in your past behavior either when it comes to potentially putting your friends in a compromising or dangerous situation, then facing the fact that you may need to make a few changes might be an order.

Since the Dangerous Liaison friend type could apply to endless scenarios, you will need to make your assessment based on past behaviors.

Think back to situations with current or former friends and consider your past behavior. Have you said or done things that made your friend uncomfortable or put them in a compromising situation?

If a specific situation comes to mind and you have an existing friend that was a part of the situation, it might be worth asking their opinion about how you behaved.

The main thing to bear in mind if you think you may have Dangerous Liaison tendencies is to be aware of how your behavior is affecting those around you. If what you are saying or doing is provocative in a way that could be conceived by others as offensive at the least and could put you or others in danger in the worst-case scenario, then stop the behavior immediately.

Meeting new people, especially those that you like can be exciting. Keep an eye on your behavior to make sure you nurture your friendships and keep them around for years to come.

# 32

## THE JUDAS

Kayla felt immediate sympathy for Trish, the new girl who had just moved to town and joined the church. The young woman in her early 20s was a recent college graduate who had moved to the area to take a new job. She sat on the church pew alone and looked around as if desperate to find a friendly face.

The women at the church tended to be cliquish and not open to newcomers. Having been in the place where Trish was now – new city and new church with no friends; was a place Kayla had found herself in only five years earlier– that had been her motivation to sit next to Trish the following week during Sunday school.

After class was dismissed and there was a short break before the main service, Kayla struck up a conversation with Trish who appeared grateful to have a friendly person to talk with. Kayla soon found that both she and Trish had a lot in common. Both had originally grown up in the state of Louisiana, worked in Human Resources, enjoyed the same tastes in music, and enjoyed going to the spa for massages and pedicures. It wasn't long before Trish had become a regular at Kayla's house, as Kayla's two-year-old son, Jeff, and husband were used to seeing Trish at their dinner table.

When Kayla discovered that she was pregnant with her second child, she was thrilled to have her new friend to share the experience. As Kayla's due date approached, she began to experience premature labor and her doctor prescribed bed rest. Trish became indispensable and was at the house around the clock preparing meals and helping out with Kayla's son.

When the day finally came for the baby to be born, Trish was right there in the labor room with Kayla's husband, holding her friend's hand. When she arrived home with her new baby daughter, Kayla was most grateful for the successful birth, her family, and her new best friend, Trish, who had proven to be reliable and an honorary member of her family.

*A few months following the birth of her daughter, Kayla was back at work. It was difficult leaving her baby girl with a sitter, but in order to maintain the lavish home she and her husband had purchased a few years earlier, two full-time salaries were required.*

*One day, Kayla's department at work held a team-building event off-site that finished up early. Kayla decided to work from home instead of returning to the office. When she arrived and saw her husband's car in the driveway, she became concerned. She entered the house and was about to head upstairs when she noticed a trail of clothes strewn on the floor that led to the family room. There, Kayla found her husband and Trish naked and spooning on the floor sound asleep.*

The trickiest part about a Judas friend is that the signs of a devious character are not always as obvious as they are in a "*Green-eyed Monster.*" The signs of a Judas can be significantly more subtle. From experience, I've discovered that a friend that fits into "*The Green-eyed Monster*" category that is not dealt with when the first signs begin to appear can eventually morph into a Judas. But like Trish in our story above, a Judas friend can appear as an extremely close and trustworthy friend, and just when you lower your guard and open the doors of trust, the Judas friend will figuratively knife you in the back.

As if the betrayal by a Judas friend is not enough, the betrayal is usually accompanied by months or years of questioning your ability to trust other people or your own judgment. I've known people who have been betrayed by a Judas friend who were never the same again and their other relationships that didn't involve a betrayal suffered as a result.

**Pros of a 'Judas' Friend**

This section was very difficult for me to write as I find it challenging to see any "pro" to having a disloyal person such as a Judas in one's life. Unlike other friend types in *Friend Encyclopedia* where I detail suggestions on how to continue a healthy relationship with the friend type, provided proper boundaries are established, when it comes to the Judas friend, in most cases, I don't believe it is possible to rehabilitate or continue a friendship with this type of a person for three simple reasons:

1. This person has betrayed you

2. In most instances, this person has destroyed your trust in an irreparable manner

3. If you do forgive them and resume your friendship, there is the strong possibility that they will resent you for forgiving them and may look for another opportunity to betray you.

Regarding reason #3 for not continuing a relationship with a Judas, I have discovered that this is almost always the case of forgiving a Judas and continuing a relationship with them. Something happens in the soul of a person who has wronged their friend and has been forgiven. It's as if the Judas knows they do not deserve to be forgiven for their treacherous act and they initially feel guilty for having been forgiven, and they don't like that feeling so they look to discredit the one they've wronged by finding fault in them to justify another betrayal.

I am by no means advocating that you should attempt retribution against a Judas or suggesting that you cannot show common courtesy or be cordial to this person. However, I strongly suggest that whatever friendship you enjoyed with this individual prior to the betrayal should be brought to a close.

At the time of this writing, there has been a warrant for the arrest of one of the "Cabo 6," the so-called friends of the late Shanquella Robinson, a beautiful and promising young entrepreneur who paid for herself and six friends to go on a trip to Cabo San Lucas, Mexico. On the evening of day one of the trip, Shanquella was killed and her friends reported to Shanquella's parents and the Mexican authorities that she had died of alcohol poisoning.

But an autopsy revealed that Shanquella had died as a result of a broken neck and not alcohol poisoning. Days after the news broke, several videos surfaced featuring Shanquella's friends filming themselves brutally beating her. Her "best friend" can be heard challenging Shanquella to fight back, and nowhere on the video is the best friend seen attempting to stop the beating or defending his "bestie."

A video surfaced on TikTok[1] that was allegedly recorded at Shanquella's funeral by a cousin who alleges that the motivation for the friends attacking Shanquella, especially the "best friend" was that Shanquella had received a PPP loan during the Covid crisis and the three businesses that she owned were thriving. Additionally, Shanquella's loan had been forgiven. The best friend had also received a PPP loan for his men's clothing business, but his business was struggling and his PPP loan had not been forgiven which meant he had to pay it back.

---

1. https://www.tiktok.com/@janedoelost/video/7175013757263940907?is_from_webapp=v1&item_id=7175013757263940907&lang=en

Envy of one's success is never an excuse to attack or harm them. One has to wonder if these so-called friends had displayed any "Green-eyed Monster" or "Judas" traits that Shanquella either didn't pick up on or ignored.

On a side note, for people who are experiencing success in life and have friends who are not experiencing the same level of success or are doing poorly, it is sometimes wise to reevaluate your relationships. While it might sound disloyal to sever a relationship with a friend as you are climbing the success ladder, especially if the friend has done nothing worthy of ending a relationship, severing a relationship at least in a tacit way is sometimes the best course of action.

The Shanquella Robinson situation is extreme in the lengths that the Judas friends went in expressing their jealousy of her. Obviously, she would have been better off to have severed ties with the six friends and made new friends that were heading in her direction.

Lesser betrayals that don't result in fatalities can still happen to the one who is experiencing success in comparison to friends who may not be doing as well.

Years ago, I developed a close friendship with an individual I will call "Joanne" that I had met at work and proved to be a Judas. I had been promoted into an account supervisor role and was experiencing phenomenal success and a lot of attention for a client. Joanne was on the same account and was overshadowed by the success I was achieving.

I had gone out of my way to share in the success and I didn't pick up on any signs of jealousy, but when a time to sabotage me presented itself, Joanne took advantage of it. I was devastated by the betrayal as I really thought of her as a good friend and we had both shared plenty of good and bad times in the workplace foxhole. It wasn't until I was betrayed by Joanne that I truly understood the expression "stabbed in the back."

I questioned everything about Joanne as well as taking myself to task for my poor judgment with regard to trusting her. I had known and worked with her for a couple of years and had put confidence in the façade of her trustworthiness.

What made it worse for me was that I was in a work situation and was forced to be around this untrustworthy person on a daily basis until I eventually left the company.

Every now and then, I bump into Joanne at a grocery store, a restaurant, or other places since we live in the same city. I am always polite and cordial during these unpleasant encounters. However, when Joanne suggests that we get together to catch up or attempts to connect with me on social networking sites, the attempts are always rejected without exception. It's not that I am still angry or bitter about the betrayal; I am not nor am I holding a grudge of any sort, but to put it simply, I will never again trust Joanne and I do not want any degree of relationship with her, period.

My experiences with Judas friends with whom I attempted to continue a semblance of a friendship eventually led to subsequent betrayals; it was inevitable. In my opinion, something happens in the mind of a Judas when he or she is pardoned and allowed to maintain a friendship with the one betrayed. It's as if the Judas now loses what little respect he or she originally had for the one betrayed and they instinctively look for another opportunity to betray.

Once a betrayal has been committed, I highly recommend cutting off the Judas.

**Cons of a 'Judas' Friend**

The cons to a Judas friend are obvious – a betrayal that can cut to the bone, and often in a manner that is very difficult to overcome. Oftentimes, a person can be betrayed in a work situation like I was or in a friendship or significant other relationship. A betrayal by someone with whom so much has been shared is always devastating. Because of the closeness of the relationship that takes place with a Judas, the profound let down of the betrayal is the number one con in this type of friendship.

Depending on the situation, a Judas friend can continue bringing hurt into the life of the person who had the misfortune of trusting this unfaithful individual. In the case of a betrayal by a Judas friend in a romantic situation as was the case in our example with Kayla and Trish, the reminder of the betrayal could be ongoing if Trish continued seeing Kayla's husband romantically and her involvement in Kayla's children's lives should Kayla's husband seek a divorce in order to be with Trish.

As stated previously, if at all possible, the person betrayed by a Judas should dissolve the friendship.

**Signs of a 'Judas' Friend**

A common trait I've noticed about Judas friends I've encountered is that they are usually personable individuals who often have a way of connecting with someone that suggests they can be trusted.

Most people desire to have someone in their life that they feel "gets them." Judas friends are usually skilled in giving off this trustworthy quality when connecting with someone. Unfortunately, it's what they do following the connection that makes a Judas a dangerous friend to have around.

Unlike a Green-eyed Monster that often verbalizes open envy, Judas friends often do not telegraph their sentiments.

Here are a few signs that you should be on the lookout for if you think you might be dealing with a Judas:

- The individual makes subtle snide remarks to you often cloaked in a joking manner.

- The individual in question makes statements in passing about unsavory interactions with other individuals. For example, they might brag about treating another person in an unfaithful manner.

- The person's reputation precedes them. If you've heard from others about something unsavory about this person, especially a betrayal, then beware!

- You catch this person in a compromising situation that doesn't lead to anything bad right away but feels like a warning.

- Your gut tells you to be on guard when you are around this individual. I strongly urge you to pay careful attention to this intuitive warning.

With regards to the last two bullets, I find that intuition about a person can often be a very reliable warning system. In my work situation where I experienced a betrayal, the first time I met my Judas friend, Joanne, I immediately felt uneasiness in my gut that she was not to be trusted, but I dismissed the gut feeling as I got to know Joanne who was very likable in the beginning.

In other situations, with Judas friends, I have felt a similar inner warning but because I genuinely liked the person, I ignored the warning and eventually paid for it.

### How to Deal with a 'Judas' Friend

Most people would not become deeply involved in a friendship with someone if they knew ahead of time that the friend would one day betray them. When it comes to dealing with a Judas friend, I'm a firm believer in taking the high road.

Accusations and screaming matches will not lessen the betrayal, and allowing a confrontation with someone who has just proverbially thrown you under a bus to escalate into a physical confrontation is the last thing you want or need.

If you find yourself in the unfortunate position of being betrayed by someone you once called a friend, the first thing you want to do is to give yourself time to process what happened before confronting the unfaithful individual.

Once you are ready, it might be a good idea to address the Judas friend directly, either in person in a safe and public environment or by phone. Since communication can be compromised in the written word such as email or text, it is best to use a method of communication that will clearly get your point across. The goal for addressing the Judas is not to reconcile with this individual so you can go back to being the same level of friends that you were before the betrayal, but to get an understanding of why the individual did what he or she did. In other words, it's to provide some form of closure to the one betrayed.

If you do not feel like you need an explanation from your Judas friend, this confrontation is not necessary.

However, I cannot stress enough that the relationship with the Judas friend should be ended, either directly or tacitly (you just don't contact them anymore and don't allow them to contact you), and no attempts should be made to reconcile with this person.

The one exception to dissolving a relationship with a Judas friend is in the case of a married couple where there is much more at stake. As was the case between Kayla and Trish, Kayla's husband was equally as guilty of the betrayal as Trish. However, if he were willing to cut off the relationship with Trish and ask Kayla for another chance, the choice to reconcile and rebuild their relationship is up to Kayla.

If Kayla chose to give her husband a second chance, however, I would still strongly recommend that she completely cut off her relationship with Trish and never attempt to reconcile with her again.

### What if You are a 'Judas' Friend?

The distinction I make between a Green-eyed Monster friend and a Judas friend is that whereas a Green-eyed Monster might subtly threaten to cross the line, a Judas friend actually crosses the line and goes to the forbidden place.

I won't pretend to understand why a person chooses to become a Judas friend. The situations I've observed as well as have been on the receiving end with Judas friends have all been different. However, the common thread I've noticed in all Judas situations is envy. Envy is never a positive element in any type of relationship. Even if an envious person never betrays their friend, the mere presence of envy degrades the relationship.

Envy is what drives a friend to become a Judas, and envy must be dealt with, head-on. Many people struggle to some degree with envy but are able to keep it under control. For the person who becomes a Judas friend, the battle to control envy is lost.

If you find yourself struggling with envy, the first thing for you to realize is that whatever areas of success you find admirable in your friend in which he or she is excelling does not diminish you in any way.

For a woman who has a friend who is physically attractive and gets a lot of attention, the envying friend might measure her looks against her physically attractive friend and feel as if she comes up short.

Or perhaps you have a friend that is excelling in his profession, recently got a promotion, and a hefty raise while you have been languishing in your job at the same level, or even worse, perhaps you just got laid off.

In the above examples, it is natural to compare the situations of others with your own, but comparisons of this nature should be avoided. If you have a solid friendship with someone, realize competition has no place in your relationship.

Even if the tables turn at some point and you are suddenly the one getting romantic attention or the one with the better-paying job or higher title, you wouldn't or at least, you shouldn't want your friend to envy you.

If, however, you do desire to have others envy you, you need to put aside those thoughts and remind yourself that there is no room in friendship for competition, whatsoever.

I realize this is all easier said than done. But as the saying goes, *"fake it until you make it."* In other words, do the right thing until the right thing feels natural for you.

While it might make you feel uncomfortable at first, if your friend is attractive, compliment him or her and say things that you would love to hear if someone were to pay you a similar compliment.

If your friend has a good relationship with a significant other or gets a promotion, compliment them or congratulate them in the same way you would like someone to congratulate you. Even if every fiber of your being wants to resist this, do it anyway, keeping in mind that shedding envy and showing true appreciation actually will feel good to you in time and will help quell the negative feelings towards your friend.

And last, keep in mind that celebrating the successes of others does not take away anything from you and in some respects, when your friend is elevated and you acknowledge it, your elevation could be right around the corner!

# 33

## FATAL ATTRACTION

*P*enny was in dire need of an attorney. Her manager at work who had always flirted with the line of decency finally crossed it and kissed Penny one evening while they were both working late. She needed to know what her rights were and turned to her friend, Blaire, for help. Blaire had previously worked for a law firm and still had contacts there. She introduced Penny to a former colleague named Leah, who was a paralegal at a respected law firm in the city where they lived.

Leah agreed to meet with Penny and invited her to come to her townhouse located in an upscale neighborhood. Upon meeting Leah for the first time, Penny was impressed with her beautiful home as well as her knowledge of workplace rules and sexual harassment. Leah took an incredible amount of time coaching Penny on how to make a list of offenses made by the manager leading up to the inappropriate kiss as well as what her next steps should be once she returned to the office the following week. Leah also arranged for Penny to meet with the managing partner attorney at the law firm where she worked and coached her on what to ask the attorney.

Penny was thrilled with the outcome of the meeting with the attorney. Her advice from Leah had paid off in a major way as the attorney agreed to take Penny's case on a contingency basis, which meant no out-of-pocket money from Penny unless he won the case. The attorney also told her that her case was quite unusual and he was very confident that the company where Penny worked would settle out of court for a hefty sum as soon as he sent a demand letter.

Penny met Leah for lunch following her meeting with the attorney and thanked her for all her help. During lunch, Leah "joked" that if the settlement was hefty enough, then Penny should give her a finder's fee. Penny thought the remark was inappropriate but laughed it off.

*As lunch was wrapping up, Penny mentioned she would be going to a job fair the following week. Leah offered to go with her to see what was out there. The request seemed a bit strange to Penny, but she agreed to it.*

*As she drove back to work, Penny received a text from Leah asking her if she wanted to have dinner that evening. That was weird. She'd just had lunch with Leah barely an hour ago.*

*Once she arrived at work, Penny texted her back thanking her for the dinner invitation but said she was going to stay in that evening. On her way home from work, Leah called Penny to see if she was still staying in or if she might change her mind about having dinner. Penny declined the dinner offer a second time.*

*She arrived home and began changing into lounging-around clothes when there was a knock on the door. Penny wasn't expecting anyone and wondered who it could be. She was shocked to find Leah standing at the door carrying bags of takeout food. What was most unnerving was that Penny had not given Leah her address.*

*Penny allowed her to come inside and the two had dinner. Before Leah left several hours later, she asked Penny about getting together the next day. Penny told her she would be busy that weekend but would meet up with her another time.*

*The following morning, the phone began ringing right at 10:00 am. Penny looked at the caller ID and saw that it was Leah. She ignored the call and allowed it to go into voicemail. The phone rang again exactly 15 minutes later; again, it was Leah. Penny turned the phone off and went back to sleep.*

*By the time Penny finally got out of bed, showered, and fixed lunch, she remembered her phone. When she turned the phone back on, she nearly fainted when she saw that Leah had called her 12 times!*

*Leah continued calling over the course of the weekend and when Penny finally broke down and listened to a few of her voicemails, she was astounded by the threatening tone of her messages. She dreaded seeing Leah at the job fair the following week.*

*On the day of the job fair, Penny arrived alone. She had not called Leah back and had ignored her many subsequent calls since Saturday. As she neared the entrance, she was disturbed to see Leah standing there.*

*Leah greeted her like nothing had happened and chatted away as they entered the building. Once inside, Leah recommended that they split up and visit different booths. She asked Penny for a few of her resumes which Penny reluctantly gave her.*

*Penny was relieved that Leah was not accompanying her to each booth, but was less than thrilled about her being there. Nearly an hour later, Penny received a text from Leah asking her to come to a particular booth. Penny went to the booth and found Leah talking with a recruiter. Leah introduced Penny to the recruiter and then excused herself. The recruiter made a snide remark about Penny having a representative. Leah's introduction had clearly not made the right impression.*

*While Penny engaged in a discussion with the recruiter, Leah began texting again. Penny ignored the texts and finally, Leah called just as another candidate stepped up to the booth. The recruiter thanked Penny for dropping by and encouraged her to answer her phone.*

*Penny was furious and left the job fair without calling Leah back and shut off her phone. Later that afternoon, when Penny pulled into the parking garage at her apartment, she wondered what she should do about Leah.*

*When she arrived at her front door, she saw that it was open. She knocked on a neighbor's door and asked him to accompany her inside her apartment in case there was an intruder. Once inside, she was horrified to find her apartment had been ransacked. There was a note in block letters left on the kitchen counter that she instinctively knew was from Leah. The letter referred to Penny as a "rude bitch" and threatened to do to Penny what had been done to the apartment if she ever stood her up again.*

While this tale between Penny and Leah may sound like the plot of a psychological thriller, something similar actually happened to someone I know. While there was no way for Penny to predict that she had just met a woman with a borderline personality, the indications rapidly unfolded right before her eyes. You'd have to wonder if Penny's friend, Blaire, might have had any insight into Leah's irrational behavior.

Oftentimes, a Fatal Attraction friend has experienced significant hurts in his or her life that compels them to behave in over-the-top ways with those they identify with as friends. Not that this is an excuse to behave inappropriately, but it is one explanation.

### Pros of a 'Fatal Attraction' Friend

Because this type of person often runs through friends quickly, they are often very skilled at winning over new people. Fatal Attraction types usually come across as very personable and accommodating. In the story with Leah and Penny, Leah essentially opened her home up to a complete stranger since she only knew of Penny through their mutual acquaintance, Blaire. Leah went out of her way to coach Penny on how to prepare for her lawsuit and what to say to the attorney at the firm where she worked. In a short time, it was off to the races for Leah whose presence almost instantly became intrusive and overbearing.

### Cons of a 'Fatal Attraction' Friend

The negative side of this friend type is obvious as portrayed in our story. Once a Fatal Attraction friend identifies and engages with a person she has decided is her new friend, it won't be long before problems begin.

It took only a few days before Leah's overbearing and disturbing ways to be revealed. It wasn't that Leah pushed the limit by asking Penny to dinner within an hour of them having lunch, but when Penny politely declined the first request (which should have been enough), Leah crossed the line by calling her after work and asking a second time and then made matters even worse by showing up at Penny's house unannounced with takeout food even after Penny had said she was turning in early and did not want to have dinner with her.

It was also inappropriate for Leah to show up at Penny's house without Penny's permission. She likely found out where Penny lived from the information Penny filled out when she signed on with the attorney, but since Penny had not shared her address with Leah, the unexpected visit was totally out of line.

I've run into this friend type a couple of times in my life and from experience, I do not think it is possible to maintain a long-term friendship with a Fatal Attraction friend without very strong boundaries in place that are firmly enforced.

### Signs of a 'Fatal Attraction' Friend

Unlike many of the other friend types in *Friend Encyclopedia* that might require you to examine closely for certain traits, the signs of a Fatal Attraction friend are obvious and lead to the same conclusion: you feel unnerved and you might even feel as if you are in danger.

Here are a few signs that you may be dealing with a Fatal Attraction friend:

- This person won't take no for an answer.

- This person crosses boundary lines that the average person would not attempt.

- Your new friend comes on very strong to the point of overbearing.

- This person pushes the limit with you and even when you set boundaries, they boldly test those boundaries.

- If you have a disagreement with this person, it is often met with hostility.

- Their constant presence weighs on you.

- You eventually feel a desperate need to get away from this person.

## How to Deal with a 'Fatal Attraction' Friend

As stated previously, setting <u>very</u> strong boundaries early on is the only way to deal with a Fatal Attraction friend. In my experience, I have found that you need to be unwaveringly firm with respect to your boundaries when it comes to this friend type. If you relax your boundaries even a little, they will take advantage.

I tend to be very low-key and casual with most people I meet but the few times I have encountered Fatal Attraction friends, I have found that this approach usually gets me into trouble as the individual with a Fatal Attraction personality will completely take advantage.

Years ago, when I entered an entanglement with a new friend that I quickly discovered was a Fatal Attraction friend, I sought guidance from an acquaintance of mine who was a practicing psychologist. When I described my new friend and her behavior, the psychologist told me that I needed to set strong boundaries immediately with this person and that I could not back down at all, otherwise, this person would completely run over me.

I took the advice and found that my boundaries had to be constantly reinforced with my Fatal Attraction friend to an extent that I didn't have to with other friends. It was a very disheartening experience because I found myself being what I would consider overly firm or even mean to this person. Unfortunately, I had to keep upping the ante and creating even stronger boundaries with this person until I finally couldn't take it anymore and had to sever ties with her.

If you find yourself in a situation with someone you suspect is a Fatal Attraction friend, you need to immediately set boundaries. You will have to determine exactly what those boundaries are, based on your situation, but here are a few examples of the types of boundaries you can set:

- *Your friend texts/calls you at inappropriate times like after midnight* – Give your friend specific time frames that they can text or call and if they violate the boundaries you set, you tell them that if it's violated again, you will block their number.

- *Your friend drops by your residence without calling first even though you have asked them not to do this* – Don't let him in and tell him that if they drop by again without notice, they will not be welcome in your home.

- *Your friend says inappropriate things that you find offensive* – Be upfront with your friend and ask them not to bring up inappropriate topics and if they do so anyway, interrupt them and don't listen. If they continue, get up and leave. If he or she is in your home, ask them to leave.

- *Your friend wants to monopolize your time in a manner that makes you uncomfortable* – If you still would like to spend time with your friend, schedule days and time limits that you will spend with them that you are comfortable with. If they push you for more time, tell them you have other obligations and this is the best you can do.

The Fatal Attraction friend is a challenging type to deal with, but if you honestly like this person and would like to remain friends with them, it's important that you set strong and clear boundaries that are mutually understood to have the best chance of succeeding in this relationship.

### What if You <u>are</u> a 'Fatal Attraction' Friend?

When we meet someone we instantly like, there can be a temptation to attempt to spend lots of time with them in a way that might seem normal to us but is excessive to them. The last thing most people want to do is offend someone they like.

If you see yourself at all in Leah or you think you might have the tendency to be overbearing with new people you meet, especially those that you like, you can decide to apply the brakes before the relationship becomes damaged.

I'm not here to judge or scold you. I know many of us meet new people every day and I understand how rare it is to meet someone with whom you feel a strong connection. If you have Fatal Attraction tendencies, then those feelings of excitement upon meeting someone you really like are often magnified.

If you have in the past behaved in a Fatal Attraction manner, think back to the things you did and think about how you could have handled yourself differently in a way that may not have turned off a friend.

If you are presently in a situation with someone and think you might be behaving like a Fatal Attraction friend, then before you reach out to that person again, think back to the past few days or weeks and the encounters you've had with this individual.

The goal here is not for you to feel bad or to beat yourself up, especially if you have just realized that you may have tendencies of the Fatal Attraction friend, but for you to make better and healthier decisions.

Let's say, for example, you have been calling someone every day, even though they are not returning your calls. Wait a minimum of three days before calling again and when you do get this person on the phone, make it a point to listen carefully to how they respond to your questions.

If you invite them to do something with you and they decline your offer, then let that be the end of the matter, and don't badger them into changing their mind. You can also follow up by asking them when a good time might be for you two to get together for a movie or some other activity.

One thing to keep in mind is that if you have been behaving like a Fatal Attraction friend for a while with this person or with others, they may feel vulnerable or a little wounded. It may take time for them to get used to you not being overbearing, so please be patient.

Realizing that you may have the tendencies of a Fatal Attraction friend is not the end of the world. Now that you know this, you can take proactive steps to curb your behavior. You may also want to consider speaking with a therapist or a behavior coach to get control over your feelings and impulses so you can better present yourself to friends and let others realize what a great friend you really are.

## 34

— • —

## CRAZY MAKER

*H*elen received a Facebook friend request from Keira, an acquaintance whom she had worked with briefly at a previous job. Helen's earlier encounters with Keira had been pleasant and she gladly accepted the friend request. It wasn't long before Keira began messaging Helen, which led to phone calls. Helen enjoyed her conversations with Keira so when Keira invited Helen to lunch, she welcomed the offer. Their first few get-togethers were amazing and Helen felt like she'd been reunited with a long-lost friend. However, there were some things about Keira that gave Helen pause. For one, Keira liked to bring up politics and start debates. These debates seemingly dragged on and on and left Helen feeling drained and frustrated. Helen told Keira how she felt about political discussions and Keira apologized, agreeing not to engage in them since they made Helen uncomfortable.

The next time Helen and Keira got together; they had an enjoyable time. When she was not bringing up politics or other social topics, Keira brought a wealth of wisdom and healthy insight to their discussions that Helen really appreciated. As they continued building their friendship, Keira began subtly slipping back into her old habits of arguing about politics.

During a heated debate, Keira suddenly lowered her voice and asked Helen why she was so upset and why she was raising her voice when she, Keira, was only asking simple questions. Keira then changed the subject to another political topic and began another argument. Helen became angrier as she began raising her voice. All the while, Keira dropped the level of her voice to a near whisper, and she looked at Helen oddly and asked, "What's wrong, Helen? Why are you shouting?"

Helen felt manipulated and decided to stop talking altogether. When the waitress came by their table, Helen gave her credit card and decided that this would be her final get-together with Keira.

Crazy Makers are people who thrive off confusion and enjoy stirring up trouble wherever they go. When pulled into a discussion with a Crazy Maker, you can be certain that the conversation at some point will turn combative where you and the Crazy Maker are on opposing sides. Crazy Makers can argue for lengthy periods without growing tired because they thrive on the negative energy generated by the arguments they instigate.

**Pros of a 'Crazy Maker' Friend**

Crazy Makers often appear to be very personable and likable people that are initially easy to get along with and are fun to be around. Their likable demeanor is what draws people into a Crazy Maker's web. Just like Keira in our story, Helen found her to initially have the demeanor of a "long lost friend" who was easy to talk with.

**Cons of a 'Crazy Maker' Friend**

"Crazy Maker" friends are constantly looking for opportunities to argue and be combative. Once they have someone on their hook, they can be relentless in stirring up strife. If you are in a relationship with a "Crazy Maker" friend, you will find yourself lured into pointless discussions that can escalate into heated arguments for no real reason. These discussions are not only time wasters but can leave you feeling needless angry, drained, and frustrated. This type can be found in platonic friendships as well as romantic relationships.

**Signs of a 'Crazy Maker' Friend**

Here are a few sure-fire signs that you are dealing with a Crazy Maker friend:

- Thrives on discussing topics that are often opposing and will escalate them into arguments.

- Usually has opposing views from yours and has no problem highlighting them.

- Will often flip the script during the argument to make it appear that you are the combative one and they are trying to bring peace.

**How to Best Deal with a 'Crazy Maker' Friend**

Once you've identified that you are dealing with a Crazy Maker, it's best to decide ahead of time that you will not engage in argumentative discussions with this person. Understand that a Crazy Maker thrives on conflict and will look for opportunities to suck you into one, so be on the alert.

Unlike the example in our story, it is not always necessary to cut ties with a Crazy Maker. However, setting strong boundaries with this person is key to being in a successful friendship with him or her. When you see yourself heading in the direction of an argument with a Crazy Maker, make it clear that you value the friendship and would like to 'agree to disagree' and not argue further. If the friend ignores your boundary and continues to argue, you will need to cut the discussion short and suggest you speak with this individual another time.

If the negative behavior persists and the Crazy Maker continues being combative, you may have to put distance between yourself and this person.

### What if You <u>are</u> a 'Crazy Maker' Friend?

If after reading the Crazy Maker description you feel you may be a Crazy Maker, this is good news! Now that you've identified a problem, you are in a strong position to take control of it. When you feel the urge to argue with your friend, especially after your friend has already asked you to not engage them in these types of discussions, simply transition the discussion to a positive topic. It can often feel exhilarating to win an argument, but when it comes to your friends and people you care for, gaining the upper hand in an argument can lead to a hollow win that can cause you to eventually lose your friend.

If you feel like you need help overcoming this urge to argue, by all means, seek the help of a professional therapist or behavior coach.

# 35

## JEDI MIND TRICKSTER

*P*amela had re-engaged with a friend of a friend she had been acquainted with years previously when she was a teenager. The friend, Sylvie, was a close friend of Pamela's cousin, Rachel. When Rachel mentioned that Sylvie and her husband had recently divorced and was back in the town where Pamela lived, Pamela was only too happy to lend Sylvie a hand.

Sylvie had moved back to the area and was out of work. Pamela had a small business and was willing to give her cousin's close friend a hand. Initially, Sylvie was excited to be working again and did a good job. However, this was short-lived and Sylvie began slacking off and complaining openly to Pamela about how unhappy she was with her role and began negatively reporting on her coworkers, even accusing one of them of stealing from Pamela.

At first, Pamela believed Sylvie and began quietly investigating the accusations. However, Pamela caught Sylvie in a couple of lies and she began to question other things she had been told. When Pamela challenged Sylvie, the woman told another lie to support the previous one. Sylvie was so adamant about her lies that Pamela questioned herself, wondering if maybe she had been wrong, even though she was certain Sylvie was lying.

After a few months, Sylvie's work performance significantly declined and Pamela realized this wasn't working. She gave Sylvie a 30-day notice that her job was being terminated. When the time for Sylvie to leave came, she stole supplies, furniture, and other valuables. When Pamela confronted Sylvie about the stolen goods, Sylvie verbally attacked with such conviction and vehemence that Pamela again questioned whether or not she was the one who had been in the wrong. Days after the incident when Pamela took a more thorough inventory of what was missing and the work that Sylvie had neglected, she realized that she had been right all along about how egregiously deceitful Sylvie had been, but how resolute she had been in her lies to Pamela.

A Jedi Mind Trickster is an emotionally damaged individual who looks for others to bend and manipulate for their gain. Jedi Mind Tricksters are experts in manipulating people into thinking their way and when caught, these tricksters will gaslight their victims to such a degree that the victim may question themselves. A common character trait of these individuals is they are often pathological liars.

### Pros of a 'Jedi Mind Trickster' Friend

Jedi Mind Tricksters are often personable individuals who start out easy to talk to and have a gift for appearing helpful and sympathetic and easily win people to their side. These are often individuals who are needy in some way and feed off of others' kindness and empathy.

### Cons of a 'Jedi Mind Trickster' Friend

"Jedi Mind Trickster" friends, once discovered, can be lethal. These individuals are chronic liars and will often lead their victims down the wrong path and engage in subversive behavior that is counterproductive to friendship. This type of friend is stressful to be around as they are deceitful and when confronted, they often behave in very volatile ways that can be unpleasant at best and violent at worst.

### Signs of a 'Jedi Mind Trickster' Friend

One of the signature moves of a Jedi Mind Trickster is that when caught in a lie, they will adamantly accuse with such conviction that the one making the accusation might question if they were the one in the wrong. Here are a few signs that you might be dealing with a "Jedi Mind Trickster":

- They constantly lie, including lying about trivial things.

- Usually have chronic emotional problems that they fail to address.

- When confronted, they will verbally and at times, physically retaliate with force to the point where the victim questions if he or she was in the wrong.

- Has very few long-term friends and is constantly making new friends that don't stick around for very long.

### How to Best Deal with a 'Jedi Mind Trickster' Friend

Strong boundaries are usually the first step in dealing with challenging friends. However, when it comes to dealing with the Jedi Mind Trickster, unless this person owns up to the wrong they have done and is willing to change, there really is no way to successfully interact with them. A professional therapist is a must for someone who is a Jedi Mind

Trickster and it is not the responsibility of you as their friend to fix them. I personally do not think it is possible to be in a long-term friendship with someone who is a Jedi Mind Trickster and is not dealing with their condition under the care of a licensed therapist.

**What if You <u>are</u> a 'Jedi Mind Trickster' Friend?**

If after reading the Jedi Mind Trickster description, you feel you may be one, take heart and make a decision to make good changes beginning today. That first change might mean getting help from a licensed professional. If you have people in your life that care about you and have allowed you to remain in their life, count yourself fortunate and do everything you can to preserve these relationships.

The first step is to acknowledge that you may have character issues that need work. Working on these issues may not be something you can tackle on your own. There is no shame in seeking help and you can often find a qualified professional who will help on a sliding scale or even for free.

Ignoring your Jedi Mind Trickster ways or projecting and blaming others for your problems will only isolate you and cause you to destroy meaningful relationships that could be mutually beneficial.

# 36

— • —

# A GOOD FFIT

I've heard many people say that there isn't a way of determining who will end up being a good friend and who will not. While there is always an element of risk in any relationship, I do believe there, definitely, are traits you can and should look for that can be an indicator. Before jumping into a new relationship with someone that you think might be a potential Full-on Friend or best friend, there is a list of five specific qualities that you should look for. If the person you are considering possesses all five of these qualities, you can consider them a Full-on Friend in Training or FFIT (pronounced "fit").

In the context of a FFIT, I am referring to a person who possesses <u>all</u> <u>five</u> of these qualities and now has the potential of becoming your Full-on Friend.

### Five Qualities of a FFIT

1. Must genuinely like you

2. Must respect you

3. Must keep his or her word to you

4. Must keep confidences (both yours and others)

5. Must be loyal

Let's review these five qualities in detail.

**Must Genuinely Like You** – This sounds like a no-brainer, doesn't it? But when I look back at my own life and reflect on the times when I'd set my sights on someone for friendship who did not particularly like me, I'm amazed at how clueless I was. When observing other people, especially adults, I'm equally as surprised by people who seek friendship with those who don't seem to like them, certainly not to the degree that the person seeking the friendship likes them.

Recently, an acquaintance of mine, whom I'll call "Diana" confided in me that a co-worker of hers was aggressively seeking a friendship outside of work. While Diana was cordial to this co-worker, she went out of her way to discourage any sort of relationship and had been reduced to ignoring voicemail messages, emails, and texts. Unfortunately, her co-worker didn't pick up on the fact that Diana did not like her well enough to pursue a friendship outside of work. Needless to say, Diana was quite frustrated in this situation.

Engaging in a new friendship must have an element of mutual like and ideally the amount of "like" should be proportionate. If the first party is strongly interested in friendship but the second party is just mildly interested at best, the relationship could be problematic. Experience has taught me that if your first impression of a potential friend does not include a mutual "like" element, it's doubtful that the like will grow in time; it is either there or it is not. And if it's not there, then move on.

If you really like a potential friend and he or she is just being friendly but doesn't like you to the same degree as you like him or her, then be careful in moving forward with this individual. I've discovered that oftentimes you will run into people who have the ability to engage easily with others in a way that they appear to be open and friendly and yet they are not as interested as the way they present. The truth about these individuals is that while many of them come across as very interested, they just happen to have the gift of engaging in a friendly manner with others also known as the "gift of gab."

**Must Respect You** – Relationships that start with "like" but never graduate to "respect" have a tough road ahead. Respect is a key element in any healthy relationship. The absence of respect can lead to future frustration not only for the individual that is not being respected but for both parties involved.

During this writing, I came across an article about a young woman who had engaged in a fight with a few of her so-called friends over Facebook, and following additional public exchanges that were disrespectful, to say the least, the young woman committed suicide.

I read through some of the messages this young woman's "friends" allegedly sent her over Facebook and I was appalled at the depth of cruelty and blatant disrespect shown through the messages.

While the young woman who took her life was obviously dealing with other emotional issues, the fact was that several of her so-called friends, one of whom was described as the young woman's 'best friend,' allegedly suggested to this woman that she should kill herself.

Words of such leveling cruelty should never be said to a stranger much less to someone with whom you have shared a close friendship. With that said, even if you and your friend are angry with one another, respect must remain intact and should be demonstrated in how you treat one another. It is possible to disagree with one another and maintain a respectful exchange.

Respect is a main ingredient in a FFIT friendship and is not something that should be turned on and off like a light switch. Respect is revealed in how a person treats you, not just how they speak to you. A person who is respectful of you rarely crosses the lines of decency, meaning they don't insult you or put you down, they don't call you names, they don't curse at you, and they don't put their hands on you in a harmful way.

When considering respect, think of how you would treat the hiring manager during an interview for a job that you wanted and do likewise.

**Must Keep Their Word to You** – When someone in your life that you consider to be a friend constantly breaks his or her promises to you, it can be frustrating, to say the least. On the flip side, when your friend keeps his or her word to you, it builds trust in your relationship. Keeping one's word is another required ingredient for a good FFIT.

When you are dealing with a person who regularly breaks their word to you, it will eventually erode the relationship and put a strain on the trust and respect elements.

I know of a man, "Phil," who had a close friend named "Dan." Dan had a habit of constantly breaking his word to Phil. While the two had been friends for more than 10 years, Phil eventually grew weary of Dan constantly breaking his word to him. In time, the two men grew apart until they were barely acquaintances.

**Must Keep Confidences (both yours and the confidences of others)** – There's a reason that governments give security clearances only to certain people who have proven themselves to be trustworthy. Some secrets need to be held in such confidence that if they were to get out, it could destroy the country.

This ability to keep confidences should be held in equal regard in your personal life and is a very important trait to watch for. Just like a government official or enlisted soldier who has been put through the rigors and has passed the tests of trustworthiness, you must first vet a potential person and they must prove themselves worthy before they are considered a FFIT.

Back in high school and even in my young adult years, I can recall having friends say to me, "*So and so told me something that I want to tell you, but you have to promise you won't say anything to anyone....*"

The problem with that was these same friends were sharing the same secret that "so and so" had told them until it really wasn't a secret anymore, since the information had been made into common knowledge.

Keeping confidences are important in building trust with a FFIT. Having a friend with loose lips who will easily share with you someone else's secrets is also something to be on the lookout for when evaluating someone you are considering for a FFIT. If that person can easily share the secret of another person, what would stop them from one day sharing your secrets?

Additionally, in many cases, there is no expiration date on confidential information that you share with others. In other words, if you confide in your friend about something and ask her to keep the information confidential, she should keep that information confidential until you tell her otherwise. Even if 10 years go by, your friend still does not have the right to reveal to anyone what you shared with her in confidence unless you give her permission to do so.

A last word on keeping confidences: Even if you and your friend have an unfortunate falling out or you lose touch, your former friend still does not have the right to break the confidences you shared with her. Confidentiality is perpetual and ongoing.

**Must Be Loyal** – Loyalty is a trait that I believe we all universally crave at the DNA level. I can't think of a single person who doesn't deeply desire to have someone in their life that they know will have their back and be their ride or die.

Many young men and women join gangs not only for the sense of camaraderie but to have individuals in their lives that they believe will be fiercely loyal to them even to the point of death.

With respect to a FFIT, loyalty where the person will stick by you no matter what (even when you're occasionally in the wrong) is a must-have trait.

So having gone over these five must-have traits to qualify a potential friend as a FFIT, you might ask yourself if you can still take on a new friend as a FFIT if he or she has most of the traits, say four out of five. While four out of five is still 80 percent, a B-minus if you will, a person who does not score a perfect 100 percent should <u>not</u> be considered a FFIT.

The FFIT is a very unique category that has the strictest guidelines that must absolutely be adhered to when considering a person to be the highest level of a friend. As mentioned at the beginning of this chapter, <u>all</u> five of these traits are present in a <u>true</u> Full-on Friend. If the person in question is someone you are considering for a different friend type, for example, a Fun Committee member or an Activity Partner, then possessing all five of these traits is not necessary, but if you are considering someone to be a FFIT or a Full-on Friend, then the person in question must possess <u>all</u> <u>five</u> <u>traits</u> without exception.

**Consider this** - if you were thinking of taking on someone for a potential FFIT who didn't seem to like you, don't you think that might be a problem?

What if this person you were considering as a FFIT didn't respect you? Or didn't keep his word, broke confidences or was disloyal? When you think about it, there really is not a single trait from the list of five that can be overlooked when considering a FFIT that one day might become your Full-on Friend. You can have someone in your life that has most of these traits or even a few of them, and they can still be considered a friend in one of the other categories, but definitely not for a FFIT or a Full-on Friend.

In case you are wondering, many people if not most do not possess all 5 traits of a FFIT. This is why having a FFIT will be a lifelong quest, and if you only meet fewer than five people in your lifetime that fall into the FFIT category, then count yourself as lucky as a true FFIT is as rare as a blue diamond!

### <u>Real</u> Friends

Many people reading this book may have what they consider to be an exhaustive list of friends. By exhaustive list, I mean they have a large number of people in their lives that they consider to be friends, but oftentimes, the hard numbers can be deceiving.

I once knew a girl who often boasted to me that she had "tons" of friends that she kept in her address book. This girl, "Adrianne" went on to explain that she had so many friends that she had to set reminders in her calendar to regularly reach out to these people, otherwise she would be overwhelmed by the sheer feat of staying in contact with everyone in her broad circle.

I was young so immediately, I took Adrianne at her word and admittedly, I was a little in awe of this individual who was so socially gifted that she had friends lining up to hang out with her.

But as I got to know Adrianne, I came to realize that it would be difficult to consider the great numbers of individuals vying for her attention to be actual friends. As I grew in wisdom and reflected on Adrianne, I realized that while she did have large numbers of people to hang out with, I would be hard-pressed to call most of them Full-on Friends or even FFITS. The majority of these "friends" were simply Fun Committee members or Activity Partners. Looking back, I would guess that of all of Adrianne's friends that I knew of, in actuality, only about three of the countless bunches were true friends, and one of the three was her sister!

### What to Look for in a Friend

Maybe you are starting a search for additional friends to add to the variety of friend types you already have. Or perhaps you've been hurt by a few people you considered to be your close friends, have isolated for a while, and now you are on the quest to rebuild your friendships. Wherever you are in your friend journey, you can start looking again with confidence that you can find good friends, provided you look in a strategic manner.

What I mean by strategic is that you look for friends using your eyes, your ears, and your gut, and not your emotions.

I know from experience that when you meet someone you sometimes want to filter out what your eyes, ears, and gut are telling you because you instantly like that person and you want it to work out. This would be considered using your emotions. We all know that ignoring the negative things that you see, hear, and sense in your gut about someone can be different from what you want emotionally, and ignoring what your eyes, ears, and gut are telling you can put you in a bad situation.

When I was in high school, I was good friends with a girl I'll call "Felicia." Felicia had just met a girl who had transferred to our school that I'll call "Kathy." Initially, I felt in my gut that there was something off about Kathy, but she seemed to be a likable person and since Felicia had hit it off with her, I ignored my feelings.

Felicia and I had a mutual acquaintance that neither of us liked named "Deanna." When I met Kathy for the first time, Felicia and I started talking about Deanna in a most unflattering way, to put it mildly. Kathy laughed as Felicia and I cracked joke after joke about Deanna and we all seemed to hit it off well.

Fast forward a few days, I was in my science class when Deanna stomped over and confronted me about what I had said to Kathy, telling me that Kathy had given her a blow-by-blow description of what I had said. It wasn't long before Deanna started swinging at me and we had a fist fight.

Later when I confronted Kathy and Felicia, Kathy boldly admitted that she had indeed told Deanna everything I had said and told me that if I hadn't wanted it told, then I shouldn't have said it.

To be honest, Kathy was right. I'm not saying that Kathy was right to have thrown me under the proverbial bus, but she was right that I should have kept my big mouth shut and not talked smack about another person in front of a total stranger who had not yet proven herself trustworthy towards me.

It is worth noting, however, that Kathy had not mentioned a word that Felicia had said about Deanna (we were both talking smack about Deanna). While I realize I was wrong for speaking ill about Deanna, in hindsight, I also realize that Kathy was a deceitful two-faced individual for going back and telling Deanna what I had said.

But the most important person to focus on in this story is Felicia. If anyone should have been using her eyes, ears, and gut in evaluating her new "friend," it should have been Felicia.

Felicia continued being friends with Kathy for a few more months following Kathy's betrayal against me. Felicia should have paid attention to what Kathy had done to me and been wary of the new girl because a couple of months later, Kathy began spreading false rumors about Felicia and the two had a falling out and stopped speaking.

As a side note, I've often thought back to what Kathy had done to me and wondered why. I have concluded that this was a case of rivalry. Kathy did not want Felicia to be friends with me and found a way to try to eliminate the competition. It didn't work. While Kathy and Felicia's friendship only lasted a few months, I continued being friends with Felicia for several years following high school.

The lesson here is when evaluating someone for a potential friendship, you need to use your eyes, ears, and gut to evaluate how they treat other people. If, like Kathy, they instigate confusion or break the confidences of others, know that this person can and may one day do the same thing to you. My grandmother used to say, "*A dog that will bring a bone will carry a bone...*" That translates to: if your new friend will betray or break the confidence of one person, they will eventually betray you or break your confidence; it's just a matter of time.

### Top 10 Qualities to be on the lookout for in a FFIT

I've put together the list below that you can use as a reference to measure your friendship qualities or the qualities of a person with whom you are beginning a friendship. While this is not by any means an exhaustive list, it can be used as a baseline of qualities to look for in a good friend.

1. The person genuinely likes you.

2. They keep their word; when a promise is given, it is kept no matter what.

3. Has proven loyalty toward you.

4. Likes spending time with you.

5. Doesn't mind you interrupting him or her.

6. Initiates plans to spend time with you.

7. Shares secrets with you and keeps your secrets.

8. Is giving and generous with you.

9. Seeks out and respects your opinion.

10. Will risk the friendship to tell you that you are making a mistake, if it means the mistake could hurt you.

On the opposite end, here is a list of 10 **negative** traits that suggests you should think twice about considering taking on this new person as a friend:

1. Tells other people information that you've shared with them in confidence, especially when you've asked them to keep it confidential.

2. Doesn't pursue a friendship with you even if you are pursuing a friendship with them.

3. Haven't passed the trustworthy and loyalty tests.

4. They're a taker who rarely gives back anything in return.

5. They regularly take someone else's side over your side.

6. Will not warn you when you are about to make a mistake and will let you do so, often telling you later that they knew what you were about to do was going to hurt you.

7. Do not defend you.

8. Makes fun of you and/or joins in when others are making fun of you.

9. Views you only as a convenience and doesn't attempt to spend time with you

unless they have no other options.

10. They're cheap with you and in comparison, they are generous with others.

By now, you should have a pretty clear understanding of the good and bad traits to be on the lookout for when considering an FFIT friend. You should occasionally review the above lists as a reminder of what you should be looking for when taking on a new friend or letting existing ones remain in your life. Keep in mind that when it comes to the practice of taking on a new friend, evaluating their character and making sure they are cleared before moving to the next step will be extremely important.

**The FFIT Security Clearance**

Too often, the personal data access gates of friendship are opened prematurely to a new person who has not yet proven their worthiness to receive privileged access to highly sensitive personal data. In other words, they are given a security clearance without having to earn security clearance credentials. As mentioned earlier, in the government and military, a security clearance is used to approve a potential government employee's trustworthiness and reliability before granting them access to sensitive information.

Certain jobs such as administrative positions, where the employee would support high-level executives and be exposed to sensitive information, or a scientist in the defense industry required to perform weapons research and development on behalf of a government require that those working in these positions are trustworthy and loyal.

The security clearance concept should definitely be applied to friendships where you might be sharing "sensitive" or "classified" personal information. Just because loose lips Laura is popular and well-liked by others doesn't mean you want to give her a security clearance into the personal details of your life.

You don't need to manufacture tests for potential friends, but casually observing your new friend, listening to what this individual says, watching what they do, and observing how they are with others will help you determine if they should be given friendship security clearance and be moved to the next level of close friendship.

# 37

## A Final Word on Friends

Hopefully, by now you have at least skimmed through all 27 friend types and have perhaps seen yourself in a few of the types and have an idea of how you might be perceived. Or perhaps, you have been experiencing trouble with a friend that fits into one of the friend types and you are now contemplating ways of dealing with that person.

One particular insight I'm hoping you have discovered from reading several of the friend types such as "Foxhole", "Holiday" and "Honorary" is that not all friendships are destined to be lifelong endeavors and some friendships have a definitive start and finish date. When the finish date comes along, it's not that either you or your friend made a mistake in being friends necessarily, but that the friendship has simply completed its course and it's time to make new friends.

It's also important to remember that one friend is not necessarily meant to serve all of your needs. For example, where you may expect a "Fun Committee Member" friend to serve your needs for a fun person to hang out and have a blast with, you probably should not expect that level of fun from a "Hidden Treasure" friend that might be a really deep person with whom you can discuss personal or confidential matters, but when it comes to the fun stuff and partying, the "Hidden Treasure" friend might be completely out of his or her element.

For this reason, I recommend you strive to have a wide variety of friend types in your life that include dependable and serious friend types like a "Hidden Treasure" and "Full-on" friends, as well as the more casual types such as "Fun Committee Member" and "Activity Partner" friends to make sure you have a wide range of friends.

In his 1966 book, *The Psychology of Science,* Abraham Maslow introduced a concept called the *'Law of the Instrument'* that states: "*When the only tool you have is a hammer, then every problem looks like a nail*[1] ."

Many people rely too heavily on one particular friend to meet their needs and this can put unduly stress on the friendship. In a sense, putting an over-reliance on one friend is like making that friend their only tool; a hammer. To avoid over relying on one particular friend, it's recommended that you maintain a variety of friend types.

For the positive and neutral friend types, you likely have a good handle on how to deal with these sorts of friends. With respect to the negative types, these may prove to be more challenging.

I am a firm believer that our friends can be among our greatest treasures and I am a proponent of a person doing all that they can to nurture and maintain friends in their life, but when it comes to the negative friend types, the day may come when you have to make a not so pleasant decision to eliminate a friend or two from your life.

One of the common threads that run through all the types of friends in *Friend Encyclopedia* is boundaries. A degree of healthy boundaries is key with all friend types including the positive types. However, the neutral and certainly the negative types often require stronger and more reinforced boundaries.

Certain friends that fit in the negative friend types will sometimes bring you to a pivotal moment of having to make a decision on whether or not to keep that person as a friend.

I call that pivotal moment that a negative friend can bring you to the "Popeye the Sailor" moment. Years ago, there was a famous cartoon series called Popeye[2] that ran in the 1960s and was replayed in syndication, even into the 1980s. Popeye was a fictitious character who was a shy, mild-mannered sailor who generally kept to himself. Popeye had an enemy named Brutus who constantly undermined him.

In nearly every episode, Popeye would always reach that pivotal moment when he'd had enough of Brutus (and sometimes other bullies) picking on him. During this pivotal moment, Popeye always said the same catchphrase: "*I had all I can stands, I can't stands no more!*"

---

1. The Decision Lab webpage description and explanation of "The Law of the Instrument" - https://thedecisionlab.com/biases/law-of-the-instrument

2. Wikipedia biography page on Popeye: https://en.wikipedia.org/wiki/Popeye

After saying that phrase, Popeye would grab a can of spinach and down it before obtaining supernatural strength, whereby he would provide Brutus or whomever a sound beating!

Not that I'm advocating physical violence of any kind, but I do believe that many of us need to experience our own Popeye the Sailor moment when we reach that place with a negative friend where we've "*had all we can stands....*"

Years ago, I experienced my own Popeye the Sailor moment when I discovered I was dealing with a "Pretender" friend. I caught this friend in a couple of epic lies and my feelings were really hurt. I had stopped returning this person's phone calls and messages for several months upon learning that I had been lied to repeatedly.

Finally, this friend sent me an email that I can summarize with: "*Look, I've already said I'm sorry, but enough is enough. If I don't hear back from you in the next 30 days, I will consider our friendship over.*"

Well, that was my Popeye the Sailor moment. I was deeply offended by my Pretender friend's letter because I felt that I needed more time to get over the hurt of learning about her lies and to figure out if I could get to that point of trusting her again, but upon receiving that threatening email, all became clear to me.

Within a day of receiving the email, I replied to my Pretender friend and said in summary: "*Let me remove all doubt for you, as far as I'm concerned, our friendship is over.*"

Did I feel any sort of regret after sending that email? You bet I did! In fact, for weeks following my response, I questioned myself as to whether I had been too impulsive or if it had been the right course of action. I had previously considered this person to be a very close friend and at the time, I wasn't sure if I had done the right thing. Months after sending the email, I found myself in a deep depression.

But those dark feelings passed. If you were to ask me today if looking back at how I had handled my Pretender friend situation and if I had done the right thing, I would say absolutely yes! In fact, if I had a top 10 list of the best decisions I've made in life, ending my friendship with this Pretender would definitely make the list.

I say all of this to make the point that sometimes you may find yourself faced with making a tough decision with one of the negative friend types.

My challenge to you is to give your situation serious thought. If necessary, pretend the situation is between two different people apart from you and the friend in question. If you knew the situation well and could advise the person who is most like you, would you tell them to remain in the friendship or would you tell them to get out of it? Let the advice that you give be the advice that you take.

Remember that not everyone you encounter as a friend is destined to remain in your life for an entire lifetime and quite often, many of the friends that we make are only in our lives for a short season.

For the friend types that are in for the long haul and are perhaps lifers such as "Hidden Treasure" and "Full-on friends, " always make sure you test those would-be long-haul friends against the qualities and traits detailed in the Good FFIT chapter before proceeding.

I hope *Friend Encyclopedia* has been of benefit to you as you move through life with existing and new friends. Once you have read the book, please review it on the Friend Encyclopedia page on Amazon .

For additional insight on the subject of friendships and many other self-help topics, visit my website at friendencyclopedia.com , sign up for my free newsletter, and check out other helpful resources. You can get in touch with me on the website's contact page or at paula@dunamispr.com, where you can ask questions or share suggestions about topics, guests, and any ideas you have about making friends or sharing a new friend type you have discovered!

Making friends is a journey and not a destination. Hopefully, *Friend Encyclopedia* will serve as a map for your journey and will help you to better navigate.

Happy friend-making!

# 38

## ABOUT THE AUTHOR

Paula Holland has been researching mind-enhancement techniques for 10 years. Her first mind enhancement program, *Mind Mansion*, was instrumental in helping clients profoundly shift their mindsets with positive results such as marriages and job promotions.

Based on her good, bad, and ugly experiences with friends, Paula decided to research and assess the types of friends she had experienced and surveyed other people and their experiences with friends. Her analysis from that research resulted in *Friend Encyclopedia*. She wrote *Friend Encyclopedia* to serve as a manual to help navigate the friend landscape to ultimately lead to happy and healthy mutually beneficial friendships. Paula lives in Northern California.

Made in United States
North Haven, CT
11 May 2024

52386357R00095